AHMED BEN BELLA

Also by Robert Merle

THE ISLAND

Ben Bella en route for his first visit as President to the United Nations (*Central Press*)

Ahmed Ben Bella

ROBERT MERLE

Translated by Camilla Sykes

With an Introduction by
Clare Hollingworth

WALKER AND COMPANY
New York

First published in the United States of America in 1967
by Walker and Company, a division of Publications
Development Corporation

Printed in Great Britain

I dedicate this book to those Africans who risk their lives daily to give meaning and substance to their country's independence.

ROBERT MERLE

CONTENTS

ILLUSTRATIONS

Introduction

By CLARE HOLLINGWORTH

The hero of the Algerian Revolution was, without doubt, Ben Bella who became one of the 'historic leaders'.

After organizing a series of incidents which culminated in a raid on the post office in Oran he was captured by the French and imprisoned. His youthful looks and smile had already captivated a large part of the Algerian people. After his escape he worked in Cairo, Tunis and Rabat and it was in a flight between Morocco and Tunisia that he was again captured by the French.

Ben Bella's years in a French prison were uncomfortable and frustrating but they gave him time to think and to learn. He emerged at the time of independence unsullied by the many minor squabbles of the revolutionary leaders and with the traditional requirement for the Presidency, wounds, prison, courage and looks.

Mr. Robert Merle, who knew him well during the period he was President, has reproduced valuable recordings made by Ben Bella during that time. In view of the *coup d'état* which replaced him in June 1965, they are historic.

My short introduction merely places them in the special French setting in which the Algerian Nationalists found themselves. I have omitted events and scenes which Ben Bella himself describes in the book.

Algiers, Alexandria, Tunis and Beirut owe much of their ancient culture and prosperity to the Mediterranean

Sea. Rome was far nearer than the desert hinterland in spirit, if not in mileage. Marseilles, Naples and the markets of Western Europe were more attractive than the caravan to Timbuktu. The geographical situation of Algeria and the whole fertile areas of the North African and Asian Mediterranean coastline have enabled the inhabitants to enjoy the benefits of two rival civilizations —those of the Christian West and the Islamic East. But the problem of how to combine both of these cultures within a smooth-running state has yet to be solved, though encouraging progress in a variety of different ways has been made in the Lebanon, Turkey and the United Arab Republic.

It is the difference of rival creeds and the ways of life they have evolved which is now at the root of the Algerian problem.

After French rule was established on the coast in 1830, the country became largely isolated from other Moslem communities. The lines of communication were all to France and it was impossible to travel along the coast of North Africa to Egypt. Between the two world wars the Algerians were virtually cut off from the active Arab nationalist movements in Egypt, Iraq, Syria and the Lebanon.

During the last war, when the Arab League was formed in Cairo, they were living under a series of military occupations, often isolated from Europe as well as from their 'Arab Brothers'.

The French settlers—*colons*—in Algeria believed that what was a golden age for them would go on for ever and the celebrations in 1930, after a century of French rule, stressed this point. But thoughtful French officials noted that little gratitude had been shown to those hundreds of Algerians who had fought valiantly and the families of those who lost their lives in the battlefields of Northern Europe.

Unless an Algerian renounced Islam, he remained in effect a second-class citizen, although the growing middle class, who were French-educated—*évolués*—were far more at ease in European than Arab society. This accounts for the fact that there have always been two types of nationalists—one, 'the assimilists' with their roots in Europe, and the other, 'the traditionalists', based on race, language and the Islamic religion.

These two factions were rarely able to agree for any length of time during the revolt and their rival philosophies have bedevilled independence.

The 'Father' of Algerian nationalism, Messali Hadj, played no active role in the revolt but it was under the cover of the underground organization that he had established that the post-war revolutionaries got together. Some of these men, including Belkacem Krim, Ben Bella and Mohammed Boudiaf, had fought bravely in the French army in the second world war. Krim sincerely believed that Algeria would be given a 'new deal' when the war was over. Instead, VE Day brought some of the worst oppressions of Algerian history in the Sétif and Constantine areas. These were followed by a series of electoral frauds.

The disillusionment which followed in 1947 caused a group of young Nationalists to form the *Organisation Secrète*, whose objective was to establish a para-military organization to sabotage French military installations. The group which included Ben Bella, then aged 28, Ait Ahmed Hocine, Mohammed Boudiaf, Lakdar ben Tobbal and Abdelhafid Boussouf managed to train a small illegal army of 300–400 men without attracting the attentions of the French. They contacted the Moslem students' leader at the University, M'Hammed Yazid, and Belkacem Krim; the latter had already formed a maquis of his own in the mountains of the Kabylia. The chief organizer was Mohammed Khider, who had been elected to the French National Assembly in 1945. He used his parliamentary immunity to help Ben Bella raise funds for the organization by means of a masked raid on the Central Post Office in Oran. This brought the O.S. to the attention of the French police and later caused them to disperse to Cairo or the Maquis. Ben Bella, their natural leader, was arrested but later escaped from Blida prison.

By 1954, these young men, tired of the quarrels of the older Nationalists, formed the Club des Neuf, the exclusive body from which the National Liberation Front —F.L.N.—grew. The members, now known as Historics, short for historic leaders, Ben Boulaïd, Didouche, Ben M'hidar, Boudiaf, Bilal, Krim, Khider, Ait Ahmed and Ben Bella, all agreed to drop their political differences and organize a revolt, to rid Algeria of the French. This revolt, the prelude to seven years of war, opened on 1st November 1954, with minor but simultaneous acts of terrorism throughout the country.

At this time, according to official French statistics, only one Algerian Moslem in ten went to school. (Naturally all the French '*colon*' children were educated.) Ninety-eight per cent of Algerian women were illiterate and 94 per cent of the men. Some 90 per cent of industry and commerce was in European hands and, for example, the *colons* owned 19,509 farm tractors, the Algerians only 418.

Fifty per cent of Algerian workers, both in the rural and urban areas, were employed for less than a hundred days each year. In addition to this chronic, almost endemic, under-employment, there was total unemployment mounting to nearly one million, with the result that many families were dependent on the remittance of the 400,000–500,000 Algerian workers in metropolitan France.

Even by 1960, when the administration was, at last, completely open to Moslems, only 5 per cent were in the top rank, 12 per cent in the second, 20 per cent in the third and 46 per cent in the fourth, where they competed with the poor whites—urban inhabitants of Bab el Oued in Algiers and similar suburbs of Oran who were even more extreme in their right-wing political views than the *colons*.

The opening of the Revolution alarmed the French authorities but not the *colons*. Indeed, the leaders themselves, most of whom ultimately gathered in Cairo, said at that time that military victory was impossible and what they hoped to achieve was to cause a psychological shock to the French and bring their case to the notice of the world. In fact, this estimate, contrary to popular belief, was the correct one. The French army, when it had, at last successfully, cut off supplies and reinforcements by closing the frontiers and driving the guerrillas to break up into comparatively small groups, could have contained the situation. They were prevented from so doing by the divisions in their own ranks and world opinion which, in turn, encouraged the rank and file of the civil Algerian population as they listened to news broadcast from Tunis, Cairo and Rabat.

The first international recognition of the Rebellion came from the Afro-Asians who invited a delegation of Algerian Nationalists to attend the Bandung Conference in April 1955. This greatly encouraged the rebel politicians who had been joined in Cairo by the 'respectable' Ferhat Abbas and Ahmed Francis. Ferhat Abbas brought with him much moderate support. He was in fact an excellent example of the French policy of assimilation. French was his mother tongue and in the now famous book he wrote in 1935, soon after his election to the Municipal Council in Sétif, he claimed that nationalism meant "the fight for our economic and political emancipation. . . . We have once and for all swept away all dreams and illusions in order to link our future firmly with France".

He was to regret those words later but, even more, those more frequently quoted, "If I had discovered the Algerian nation, I would be a nationalist and I would not blush for it as a crime. Men who die for patriotic ideals are honoured and respected. My life is not worth more than theirs. But I would not die for an Algerian fatherland because such a Fatherland does not exist. I questioned history. I questioned the living and the dead. I searched through the cemeteries; nobody could speak to me of it. You cannot build on air."

Ferhat Abbas was to become a sincere if not violent Algerian nationalist but he realized that his country's economic prosperity must, in the foreseeable future, depend on France and he has been severely criticized by the more militant groups for this.

Naturally, owing to their clandestine activities and the sometimes insurmountable problems of communication, major differences of opinion arose between those who were fighting inside the country, often in isolated mountains, and the men—Exteriors—operating from Cairo.

From the beginning the old Turkish administrative areas—the *willayas*—had been used as rebel units. There were six of these and sometimes Algiers was treated as an autonomous seventh unit but at others it was incorporated in *willaya* IV.

In the summer of 1956, it was decided, apparently

without the knowledge of Ben Bella, to hold a conference inside Algeria to be attended by representatives from all the *willayas* and the Exteriors. Despite overwhelming problems of security, the meeting took place in the Soummam Valley in 1956. Members of the 'Exterior Delegation' were unable to attend as the place of the meeting had been changed at the last minute because the French authorities had captured some papers which could have given away the site of the earlier meeting-place.

Representatives of three of the six *willayas*—North Constantinois, Kabylia and Algerois—spent three days in a disused army hut and thrashed out their policy with trade union leaders. Indeed, 250 leading rebels who met under the nose of the French army decided to set up an overall Executive and Co-ordinating Committee and a National Council of the Algerian Revolution, to be composed of representatives from all over Algeria to act as the final charged executive authority for the Revolution.

The brain behind this was Ramdane Abbane. Unfortunately, again owing to the difficulties of communication these decisions did not become known to the Exterior Delegation for several months. Some observers believe that Belkacem Krim was the organizer but I think he as well as the other historic leaders were jealous of Ramdane Abbane.

Had Ben Bella not been arrested at this time, an open split in the ranks of the F.L.N. would have been impossible to avert. Although Ramdane Abbane died later in mysterious circumstances, the differences between the supporters of Ben Bella—already imprisoned in France— and the men of Soumman were not to die.

By 1956 both Morocco and Tunisia had become independent and many of the 'externals' moved to Tunis. Inside Algeria a young bespectacled chemist, Youssouf

Ben Khedda, organized a network of terrorists in the Casbah of Algiers, the walled city within a city to which the Internal Executive Committee had moved. In October 1956 the battle of Algiers, which was nothing more than indiscriminate urban terrorism, but on nothing like the scale the Jewish terrorists practised in Palestine, opened and almost brought the life of the city to a standstill.

Robert Lacoste, who had been appointed 'Resident Minister' in 1956 by the Socialist Premier, Guy Mollet, misguidedly handed over police powers to the French army when terrorism was at its height in Algiers. Thereafter civilians were sharply told not to interfere or inquire into the methods used by the army.

Finally, General Jacques Massu and his battalions of paratroops, through overwhelming force and the use of torture, managed to arrest the last of the F.L.N. terrorist leaders in 1957.

The organizers claim that the publicity that the battle achieved in the United States and Europe, combined with the sympathy which it evoked amongst the Moslem population of the city—then around 450,000—justified the loss of life.

The battle of Algiers depleted the ranks of the F.L.N. and soon after it the construction of vast electrified barrages sprinkled with minefields made the guerrilla's task ever more difficult. French helicopters regularly patrolled these installations which I saw on many occasions, and it is difficult to believe the Algerians one meets in the Aletti Hotel Bar today who claim they crossed it several times. Nor was the sea route much easier, owing to the constant patrols of the French navy and air force. However, small boats were landed from time to time in or near the charming resort of Dellys in the Kabylia.

As the Rebellion mounted in intensity and attracted increasing publicity in the world's press, so the attitude of the million, three hundred thousand Europeans in Algeria hardened. A few brave characters in all walks of life from the big land-owners to the French postman, followed the example of the Mayor, Jacques Chevallier, and the excellent priest at Bab el Oued, Father Scotto, and made efforts to keep the two communities from civil war.

But the vast majority of Europeans knew they were fighting for a way of life they could never hope to enjoy again. The wife of the 'poor white' of Spanish communist extraction who walked to market in a soiled dressing-gown, followed by an Arab maid to carry her parcels, was a common sight. Their verbal violence knew no bounds. A hairdresser in Oran seriously proposed that if we (Europeans) all killed fourteen Algerians the problem would be solved. And she added, "I am willing to kill them with my strong bare hands."

The intemperance of the 'poor whites' was the driving force which led ultimately to the change of mind on the part of liberal-minded French officials and the more moderate businessmen and landowners. One after another Delegate or Resident Minister—the title of the senior French official changed—was gradually brought round to the viewpoint of the French Algerians. The Europeans on the spot knew they could make or break officials. Jacques Soustelle went to Algiers as a left-wing Gaullist but the sight of atrocities perpetrated by the rebels and the warm treatment he received from the French Algerians converted him to their viewpoint. Lesser characters fell more quickly into the French Algerian net.

Lacoste, the Resident Minister, was aware that there were plenty of plots designed to overthrow the French government but both he and the army were taken by surprise when Pierre Lagaillarde, wearing the uniform of a French 'para' officer and his following of European students charged the steps by the War Memorial that led to the Forum—a vast space in front of the main French administrative buildings—and after a series of demonstrations they entered the offices and amused themselves by tearing up thousands of files.

The Commander-in-Chief, General Raoul Salan, was conveniently out of town and General Jacques Massu was therefore responsible for public safety in Algiers. He misguidedly, but understandably as he could obtain no orders from the French capital, agreed to the establishment of a Committee of Public Safety.

The demonstrations, which could never have taken place on this gigantic scale without the tacit consent of the French army, gradually developed into a mass movement demanding the return of General de Gaulle to power. It was these demonstrations in Algiers on 13th May which led, albeit indirectly, to the overthrow of the Fourth French Republic.

The Europeans and army alike had no doubts that the General supported Algérie Française—a French Algeria. They knew, too, that he was the strongest man in France and the only one capable of enforcing this policy. The demonstrators were joined by Moslems—some of whom were no doubt rounded up by the Paras—who joined the cry of "de Gaulle to power". Demonstrations continued on a minor scale until de Gaulle assumed power as Prime Minister in Paris on 1st June. Soon afterwards he made a triumphant tour of the country in which the Europeans —Pétainists almost to a man in World War II—turned out to give him massive support, encouragement and adulation.

No one appeared to notice that he said little or nothing about his future policy. The words chanted by the crowds, "Algérie Française", only passed his lips once—in Tlemcen. In Algiers he uttered the somewhat cryptic phrase to a massed audience of Europeans and Moslems, *"Je vous ai compris"* (I have understood you). So he had: but they did not then realize this fact. De Gaulle made it clear that there would be no going back on the past and said in future in Algeria there would be only one category of inhabitants—"Frenchmen in the full sense". The referendum held in France and Algeria to legalize de Gaulle's return to power resulted in a 96·7 per cent in favour of the new leader. Moslem women voted for the first time but it was all rather a 'picnic' as crowds of Moslems from the Bled were taken to the polling booths by the French authorities.

De Gaulle appeared to concentrate on improving the economy of the country and announced the Constantine Plan, designed to create nearly half a million new jobs.

During the next few months the more extreme officers were removed from Algeria, including General Salan, the C.-in-C. It was perhaps the lowest ebb of the Revolution but Arab terrorists began at this time to operate on a small scale in metropolitan France. They were still severely hampered in their operations in Algeria by the effective sealing of the frontiers with Tunisia and Morocco and the vast 'pacification' programme which had been started under the Soustelle régime. Hundreds and thousands of villagers were removed, often by force, from their scattered mountain villages to resettlement areas which were easier for the French authorities to control. These new villages varied in style from camps surrounded by barbed wire, where bored French officers watched crowds of listless Arabs throughout the day, to well-constructed settlements where French officers enthusiastically trained men for new jobs and assisted them in building schools and medical centres.

After independence, thousands of Arabs remained in their new villages, in many cases because their old homes had been destroyed but also because they had grown accustomed to running water and even to electric light. The inhabitants of the new settlements were all collecting funds secretly for the F.L.N. Sometimes the picture of Ben Bella—less frequently Ferhat Abbas—was hung beside the official one of General de Gaulle. Ben Bella's name, although he was in a French prison, was a household word: the only leader's name known to the Moslem women except, perhaps, in the Kabylie where Krim was the local hero of the revolt.

The G.P.R.A. (Provisional Government of the Algerian Republic in Exile) under the Premiership of Ferhat Abbas was already established in Tunis when de Gaulle made his offer of 'a peace for the brave'. The rebels saw it only as a trick to get them to lay down their arms; the Europeans as the beginning of a betrayal by de Gaulle. Nothing happened and the new French President was not surprised: it was apparently merely a part of his softening-up process.

Late in 1959, Paul Delouvrier, an economist who had been appointed Delegate-General to Algiers, was trying to pave the way for a policy of 'self-determination'. But it did not require the Deuxième Bureau to discover that plots, this time against de Gaulle, were being made in both Algiers and Paris. Senior French officials as well as army officers staunchly refused to implement Delouvrier's policy.

A newspaper interview given by General Massu sparked

off the first show-down between de Gaulle and the Europeans. Massu was immediately transferred. The extremist political groups who had already reformed under Joseph Ortiz, a café-owner, and Pierre Lagaillarde, began demonstrations which soon led to rioting. Some of the French troops refused to fire on the Europeans who barricaded themselves in a block of streets which included some university buildings in the centre of the town. After the first few days the insurgents, who were fed by the army and their many friends in the population, became something of a joke and life went on normally in the rest of the city. Ortiz escaped and Lagaillarde gave himself up to face a trial. They had both failed in their attempt to force the army to come to their support: this failure naturally strengthened de Gaulle's hand. Soon afterwards the President flew to Algeria and once more in July repeated his peace offer.

As a result, Maitre Ahmed Boumendjel (later to become spokesman for Ben Bella) went to talk with French representatives at Melun. It was unfortunate that Boumendjel was not allowed to meet the press nor any of his French friends. He felt and indeed was a prisoner and the contact ended in failure.

Meanwhile, from a modest house in Tunis the G.P.R.A. were making a considerable impact on the Anglo-Saxon press. M'Hammed Yazid, the Minister for Information, was particularly effective in publicizing the support they were receiving as Ferhat Abbas visited Mao Tse-Tung in China and the Arab leaders while no one talked about the Algerian army which was being armed and well trained on Tunisian soil by Colonel Houari Boumedienne. The Colonel was one of the few Algerian rebels to speak Arabic as his mother tongue because he had been educated largely in Cairo. He was pale and uninspiring to look at but he displayed considerable ability as an organizer and administrator. Indeed, the Algerian army in exile was to become so strong that the President of Tunisia, Habib Bourguiba, feared Boumedienne might attempt to overthrow him because the Tunisian army was, and indeed still is, negligible. Fewer people can have prayed more fervently for Algerian independence than Bourguiba who, for considerable periods, was hardly even on speaking terms with the relatively harmless political members of the G.P.R.A.

Inside Algeria the French army had some 400,000 men who had learnt how to deal with rebels and dropped much of their heavy equipment while, at the same time, they had developed the use of helicopters for reconnaissance and transport purposes and to provide covering fire to the troops when necessary.

It was this powerful, almost successful army force that caused the next round of trouble for de Gaulle. Alarmed by the intention of the French government to come to terms with the rebels, four French generals organized a *coup d'état*. At 7 a.m. on 22nd April, the Algiers radio announced that "the Armed Forces" had taken over Algerian territory ". . . according to plan and without a shot". A state of siege was declared and General Challe (former Commander-in-Chief in Algeria) announced that he and Generals Zeller, Jouhaud and Salan had acted "impelled by their oath to keep Algeria French".

The *coup* was executed during the night by the tough men of the 1st Parachute Regiment from Zeralda. The Delegate-General, M. Jean Morin, and a visiting Minister, M. Robert Buron, were overpowered in the Summer Palace when the troops disarmed the police and took control of all public buildings.

The senior Admiral refused to join until he knew what political support the insurgents had in Paris. But General Bigot, commanding the Air Force in Algeria, rallied and only a sandstorm which blew up after the paras had enplaned appears to have prevented their attempt to drop on Paris and take control of the French capital.

On 23rd April, President de Gaulle announced over radio and television networks that he had "taken over full powers" under Article 16 of the Constitution. Most Frenchmen then turned off their sets and went to bed but, later, the Prime Minister, M. Michel Debré, announced that an air-borne descent on Paris might be imminent. The Prime Minister was made something of a laughing-stock for over-dramatizing the situation. But the un-popular M. Debré, when he spoke, did know that the aircraft were waiting with engines running on Maison Blanche military air base for visibility to clear before take-off.

The European inhabitants were delighted by the *coup*, General Challe called for further concentrated action against the Algerian rebels and Salan took over the civil administration. Behind the scenes, the European revolt soon lost momentum as commanding officers delayed joining until they could obtain an answer to their vital question: "Where are the troops' pay and rations coming from when the limited supplies held in Algeria are exhausted?"

The conscripts are generally built up as the heroes who stood by de Gaulle but, in fact, it was practical issues which fostered this loyalty to the President.

By midnight of April 25–26, the radio station in Algiers resumed normal transmissions. At 2 a.m. General Challe gave himself up and was flown straight to Paris to face a trial on insurrection charges which carried the death penalty and General Salan and his brilliant intelligence officer, Colonel Godard, went into hiding with arms and military support to form the O.A.S.—Secret Army Organization—which later caused as much, if not more, havoc in Algeria than the Algerian rebels.

M. Louis Joxe, an intellectual Gaullist, who had taken cabinet responsibility for Algeria, flew across the Mediterranean with General Olie to restore order whilst Paris concentrated on the early resumption of peace talks with the Algerians. There were semi-official rumours that the *coup* had received some sort of official blessing from the C.I.A. in Washington. Meanwhile, 220 officers in Algeria were relieved of their commands and 200 officials of their posts, but in the lower grades government action was still sabotaged as many of these humble 'functionaries' began working for General Salan.

One of their first acts was a plan, which was discovered before it could be put into effect, to set fire to the Casbah, the old walled native quarter of Algiers, by blocking the narrow entrances, starting fires simultaneously and preventing the population from getting out. It was an effort to prevent the Evian peace talks opening. Jaques Coup de Frejac, Director of Information, played an important role both in Algiers and during the peace talks at Evian. With the advantage of hindsight and in contrast with the attitude of many officials in similar posts in Whitehall today, 'Coup' did a wonderful job.

General de Gaulle fully realized the increasing support amongst the Moslems of all classes in Algeria for the rebellion. During his visit to Algeria in December 1960, I witnessed demonstrations in which the Moslems and Europeans took part and the former drowned the shouts of "Vive de Gaulle" with cries of "Algérie Algérienne". The crowds came to blows in Ain Temouchent and

Orleansville and were only parted by troops and gendarmerie. Demonstrations in the suburbs of Algiers ended with the stabbing of Europeans and the Casbah, which had been calm for months, suddenly became the scene of wild demonstrations in which the Algerian rebel flag —green and white with a red star and crescent—was unfurled.

The first phase of the Evian talks broke down, officially, because M. Louis Joxe, the leader of the French delegation, said, "I will talk to the M.N.A. (the party of Messali Hadj) as well as the F.L.N." But there were other reasons. The Algerian delegation, which was housed on the outskirts of Geneva, in a large villa owned by one of the rich Gulf sheikhs, was led by Belkacem Krim, then 'Foreign Minister' of the government in exile. Ahmed Francis, a doctor, the brother-in-law of Ferhat Abbas and 'Finance Minister' together with a former terrorist Saad Dahlah and Maître Ahmed Boumendjel made up the delegation. They all complained of undiplomatic treatment from Joxe who, it was said, had spittoons specially put out for them. The French government still hoped for some kind of 'association' with Algeria and the right to retain sovereignty in the Sahara where the rich petroleum and natural gas deposits were being exploited.

Late in June 1962, the Evian Agreements were finally signed on the assumption that the majority of the Europeans would remain in the country and that after the referendum on the country's future—which it was agreed would be held in Algeria—independence would be "in close association with France".

Ben Bella, who had by this time been moved to a comfortable prison château in the Loire Valley, and President de Gaulle both agreed the full text of the Agreement, much of which was obsolete before its terms could be implemented. The French were to retain the right to use bases and nuclear testing sites in the Sahara for fifteen years as well as the air base at Bône and important naval base at Mers el Kabir. Algeria was to remain in the franc zone: it has been of great benefit to the new state to do so. After the cease-fire, an Algerian Provisional Executive would administer the country through the interim period while the referendum was organized and until the new government took over.

A Moslem, Abderrahman Fares, former President of the Algerian Assembly, was appointed President, with a team of mixed Moslems and Europeans. They were to occupy offices in Rocher Noir, the modern administrative city the French government had built outside Algiers by the sea. They had hoped that this isolated location would prevent French officials from falling under the influence of the *colons*. Rocher Noir was hardly used and it is now the home of Russian and Czech technicians who are training Algerians in engineering and other technical skills.

Fares never had a chance.

The whole of the last spring and summer of French rule in Algeria was taken up by the activities of the O.A.S. whose members established an underground headquarters in the cities of Algiers and Oran in order to carry out their ruthless sabotage and destruction. Their illegal contacts with the army remained good and their intelligence network was excellent. The O.A.S. terrorists supplied with arms and money from their European sympathizers were able to move around as Mao Tse-Tung advised, "not noticed", like fish in the sea.

There were many occasions when the French authorities appeared to be allowing them to get away with it. Air-France refused to accept passengers unless they obtained an O.A.S. permit to leave the country. Telephone communications to Europe were only given either to O.A.S. sympathizers or those who paid enormous bribes. More serious, thousands of Moslems were driven from their shops and offices by plastic explosions which rarely completely destroyed property but made it uninhabitable.

I saw O.A.S. agents 'arrest' men in the Aletti Hotel in full view of French officers who refused to intervene. The number of people killed in the major incidents in the Rue d'Isly and Place du Gouvernement amounted to over a hundred but it was the daily bomb that wore the population down.

After General Salan was captured on Good Friday, the desperate men grew even more bloodthirsty. They appeared determined to destroy the country they could no longer rule. But they realized the end of their power was in sight.

As a result of the good offices of M. Fares and the former Mayor, Jacques Chevallier, a cease-fire was secretly negotiated between the F.L.N., represented by Dr. Shawki Mostefai and a somewhat dubious character in the O.A.S., Jean Jacques Susini. It was not fully kept by the O.A.S. but from that moment the Europeans were encouraged to leave for France. From 20th May the French authorities set up a round-the-clock airlift to handle the traffic at Maison Blanche, Algiers.

On the Algerian side, Ben Bella was released—his own account of these events is related in this book.

A month after the triumphant entry of Ben Khedda, Ben Bella moved into Algiers. The G.P.R.A. had by that time virtually disintegrated and Ben Khedda recognized the supremacy of the Political Bureau. Independence is fully covered in this book.

There is little doubt that Ben Bella was staking a great deal on the second Afro-Asian Summit Conference which was due to take place in Algiers in June 1965. A former exclusive resort, the Club des Pins, had been transformed into an enclave for the conference. A huge hall had been constructed, roads, restaurants, bars and hotels.

Just before it was due to open, Ben Bella was overthrown by a *coup d'état* headed by Colonel Boumedienne. A few shots were heard in the night at the modest Villa Joly which Ben Bella made his home. Since that day, no one has seen him though his mother is said to have received a letter in his handwriting.

The day after the *coup*—19th June—Colonel Nasser sent a strong delegation, headed by the Vice-President, General Amar, to demand to see him. Indeed, Ben Bella's disappearance was largely responsible for the fact that the conference was postponed until the autumn.

It never took place at all.

As soon as the news of the *coup* reached the countryside, women especially began to demonstrate against Boumedienne. In Algiers they rushed from the Casbah into the main street shouting in Arabic: "Long live Ben Bella" and "Boumedienne to the gallows". There was some effort on the part of the trade unions to join them but this failed through cowardice.

Boumedienne has now been in power for a year and still Algerians are uncertain what his political objectives really are. He has changed little since the *coup* but the country has continued to run downhill economically. If the Algerian dinar were not backed by the French franc, the situation would be beyond imagination. For a time, Boumedienne attempted to persuade former known rebels such as Ferhat Abbas to join him, but no one was willing to take the plunge.

The streets are still cleaned and the dustbins emptied, but the economic life of the country is slowly moving towards a complete standstill. The 'nationalization' of several foreign firms has frightened the rich international companies who were considering further investments in the petroleum industry.

In spite of good harvests, agricultural production is low—how low no one knows because no statistics have been kept since French officials left the country. Colonel Boumedienne is likely to remain in power just as long as the army is well-fed and well-paid. For this he is dependent on France. But conditions may become so bad throughout the country that he will be driven to hand over political power to those former leaders who earlier refused to join him on *his* terms. The only possible effective discontent is in the air force but, although they have weapons and personal drive, it is difficult to envisage them organizing another *coup*.

Some Western diplomats were cheered by the Boumedienne *coup*. Ben Bella, they feared, was too friendly with Cuba and other dangerous régimes of the left. Boumedienne, they believed, because he was religious, would be more inclined to the West.

A few organizations have closed down, such as the Algerian-Cuban Friendship League. There has been a purge in the civil service but otherwise Boumedienne has offered a bewildered poverty-stricken people all too little.

During the past few months there have been sporadic demonstrations against the new ruler but even these seemed listless and half-hearted. Algeria will one day find its own personality and government. Let us hope, for the sake of the miserable, disillusioned people there, that it may be soon.

Preface

I first met President Ben Bella in February 1963 at Sidi-Ferruch, at the *Centre des Petits Cireurs*.[1] The boys had just been brought there by bus. My wife and I mixed with the training staff and, from first shower to final outfitting and from there to the dormitory, we followed the whole process of transformation of those wretched filthy *yaouleds*[2] into clean little boys in new blue overalls.

I remember their first sight of the new dormitory full of white beds; it gave them a kind of shock. They did not dare to sit on the beds or even go near them, in spite of the staff urging them on with: "Come on now, don't be afraid—this is where you are going to sleep."

It was *Ramadan*,[3] so we had to wait until sunset, when the fast was broken and the children brought into the refectory. A delicious-smelling bowl of *chorba* steamed in the middle of each table. The former shoe-shine boys sat round the bowls in silence waiting to be served, their black eyes fixed on the soup with an expression of eager concentration.

It was at this moment that Ben Bella arrived, accompanied by Boumedienne and Boumaza, in a cavalcade of black Citroëns preceded by motor-cyclists. There ensued in the refectory a busy, cheerful bustle in which ministers

---

[1] Tr. note: a rehabilitation centre for the shoe-shine boys of Algiers.
[2] Tr. note: North African Arabic for boy or urchin.
[3] The yearly fast observed by Moslems from sunrise to sunset, and which lasts for thirty days.

were caught up with motor-cyclists, because their arrival coincided with the end of the fast, and hospitality demanded that they should immediately be offered biscuits and fruit. I can still visualize the eagerness with which the famished outriders, having shed their crash-helmets, flung themselves down at a table and devoured the simple dishes which they were offered. There is a subtle but somehow healthy voluptuousness in this fast as practised; everything is forbidden during the day, but at nightfall food, drink, cigarettes and love are once more allowed. In this way, the sharpness of desires which only become legitimate at night is heightened by the imagination during the day.

Amongst the happy throng of men who had broken their fast after a hard day's work, the shoe-shine boys had for the moment been forgotten. They still sat speechless round the *chorba* bowls, their empty plates in front of them. With the help of my wife, I started to serve them and it was at this moment that Ben Bella saw me and immediately came towards me. I introduced myself, he said a few pleasant words to me about my writing and then added laughingly: "I mistook you for some foreign ambassador—the thing is, they seem to arrive every day, and I spend my time meeting them!" Then he began to talk to me about the shoe-shine boys, and I was immediately struck by his sincerity and his modesty. He said that he had no illusions on the outcome of this experiment, and that a lasting solution was still to be found. He repeated: "This is only a beginning, a very small beginning. But we will go on."

Several months later, he invited me to lunch at his house, the Villa Joly,[1] together with an Algerian friend.

[1] At the top of the Boulevard Salah-Bouakir (the former Boulevard Télemly) almost opposite the splendid Palais d'Eté, stands the Villa Joly, surrounded by walls. A four-

No head of state can ever have been as simply housed as Ben Bella, with the possible exception of Fidel Castro at Havana, where the only luxury is a terrace opening out of his small studio, which he has had equipped for gymnastics and basket-ball.

I had a long, interesting and animated conversation with Ben Bella. There was much talk of Cuba, from where I had just returned. Ben Bella spoke of his warm friendship for Fidel and, as I listened to him, I was struck by the pragmatical way in which he too foresaw the evolution of his own country. The evidence was that this second generation of great revolutionary leaders, unlike the first, was not overconcerned with questions of doctrine.

Ben Bella also recalled some episodes of his life in the French army during the Italian campaign. As I listened to him, I thought to myself that we really knew very little about this man who, because of his personality and the strength of his convictions, had been called upon to become a great African head of state and unquestionably one of the leaders of the Third World. After a moment, I asked him whether, if the opportunity should arise, he would give me his life story. To this he agreed.

A few months later, in spring 1964, Ben Bella sent for me. It was agreed that our conversations should be tape-recorded in order to save me the labour of taking notes. There were in all fifteen of these sessions, each one lasting two to three hours. Ben Bella was invariably calm and smiling, never tense and never impatient. It was never he who ended these sessions; with his scrupulous peasant

storey building with bright sunny rooms but not in any way luxurious, the Villa Joly used to be occupied by government officials. From the security point of view, the house seemed badly protected. One of its walls looked down into an alley, and police protection for the President of the Republic amounted to only three men.

politeness, he always left the initiative to me. The interviews were at first rather difficult, as my interlocutor had a habit which disconcerted me until I knew its cause; he would never mention a name or a date, like all people who have spent a great part of their life in hiding.

There were other, deliberate omissions which Ben Bella explained to me when we came to them. He told me that he did not wish to speak of the internal affairs of his government, of his contentions with Morocco, or of the Kabyle revolt, as he wanted in all cases to reach a state of reconciliation. In the last chapter, therefore, Ben Bella does not, of necessity, cover all aspects of Algerian politics from 1962 to 1965. But the most important and fundamental work of his government, *autogestion*,[1] is given all the earnest attention that it demands.

At the time of these interviews Ben Bella was forty-six, in fine physical shape and much younger-looking than his age. Big and well-built, rather heavy and full-faced, there was something youthful and trusting about him, particularly in the openness of his smile, which one did not expect to find in a statesman. One was simultaneously aware of his courage, of a natural dignity, and of the unpolished forthrightness of the *fellah*. He spoke French fluently, with a few inaccuracies and a slightly rugged accent, but also with a pungency and a vigour which some of his better-educated compatriots had lost. He had been unable to pursue his studies further than the *brevet* stage and he was largely self-educated, having learnt far more from political combat than from books. Intelligent and frank, a devout but not fanatical Moslem, essentially

---

[1] In April 1963, the important firms and agricultural concerns belonging to Europeans were nationalized. They were not, however, taken over by the State, but were left to the management of the workers and employees (assembled in a *Comité de Gestion*) who were already working on them. The workers gave themselves a monthly salary and a share of the yearly profits.

2

Arab, but without the xenophobia[1] so rife in official circles at the moment, his approach seemed remarkably human. If he was not assassinated on the 19th June 1965, and if the present government eventually allows him to have the trial which they have so frequently announced and then postponed, it will be very difficult to accuse Ben Bella of having shed Algerian blood. Under his government there was only one execution, that of Chaâbani, an indefensible character whose terrorist gangs had made him hated by the whole population.

Ben Bella played an important part in the preparation and launching of the Algerian Revolution. There is no doubt that he deserves to be known, as he and his followers have claimed, as an 'historical leader'. During the Revolution he took over a very important armaments organizing task, and the *willayas*[2] were the first to suffer by his capture. It became obvious after that, that nobody in the ostentatious *Extérieur* and G.P.R.A. was going to concern himself overmuch with the fighters of the *Intérieur*. After the Declaration of Independence, in spite of some wavering and at the cost of some mistakes, he worked loyally towards carrying out the Tripoli programme, fought against speculation and middle-class Moslem machinations, and laid the foundations of agricultural socialism in Algeria. By taking up an uncompromisingly clear position in African affairs, in a short time he brought international prestige to his country.

The *coup d'état* of the 19th June, with its catalogue of

---

[1] This xenophobia is, moreover, capable of distinctions. If it includes Egyptian schoolteachers who are now considered to be 'useless', and dedicated Bulgarian doctors now described as 'just good enough to be male nurses', and if it explains the recent arrest of harmless young Frenchmen loudly denounced as opposition ringleaders, it does not for all that rule out business relations with Federal German industrialists.

[2] F.L.N. troops were divided into *willayas*, corresponding to the different natural regions of Algeria, and enjoying considerable independence. These military regions did not necessarily correspond to the 'departments'; for instance, *willaya* IV was the *willaya* of Algiers, but did not include the whole of the department.

libel and blackmail, arrests and shootings on public high-
ways, of secret torture and hushed-up executions,[1] struck
me from the very first day as being a *cuartelazo*[2] in
classical South-American style. In this connection, it is
very characteristic that the military *junta* which seized
power by the sword has not once discussed the possibility
of a referendum, which would give the Algerian people
a say in their future. In spite of the strong police force
at their disposal and the Algerian colonial tradition of
rigged elections, the conspirators have not yet dared to
summon the people to the polls to give their action a
semblance of legitimacy. The conspirators themselves
know that the restitution to their former owners of certain
properties taken over by the people, and the subtle
sabotaging of *autogestion* by the non-payment of salaries
leaves them little chance of victory in a free election.

Their attitude in other respects continues to cause
grave speculation as to Ben Bella's fate. Immediately
after the 19th June, I felt sure that he had been murdered
on the night of the *coup d'état*, as that would be a crime
well fitting the mentality of those who organized the
cuartelazo. Since then, Boumedienne and his ministers,
while referring to Ben Bella with the greatest hatred in
their public speeches, have asserted on many occasions
that he is still alive. I was staggered by these assurances
without being entirely convinced of their truth. If Ben
Bella is alive, why has no reliable witness such as an
Arab diplomat or a European lawyer been allowed to see
him since the 19th June? By allowing this, it would be
so easy for Boumedienne to clear himself, once and for
all, of the odious suspicion that (like Tshombé) he has

---

[1] For instance, who knows what has happened to Nekkache, the Minister of Health?
It was announced that he had been wounded in the course of arrest. Has he died of his
wounds? Is he still alive? And if so, where is he?
[2] A military coup.

hoisted himself to power by the assassination of his rival.

Assuming that Ben Bella was killed during the night of the 19th June, it is easy to see why the conspirators, rather than face violent popular reaction, should have preferred not to reveal the fact of his death at the time, and that they should have decided to postpone the announcement to a time when their own position was more secure and feelings were calmer. The myth of Ben Bella's imprisonment would then be built up by means of newspaper articles, press conferences, and false reports leaked to journalists, until the day when Boumedienne's government, feeling itself stronger, would tell the world that Ben Bella had succumbed to illness in his prison cell, or that he had committed suicide, or that he had been fatally wounded while trying to escape. . . .

In any case, the mystery will have to be cleared up sooner or later. I hope with all my heart that my foregoing theory is false. I hope, though without much conviction, that Ben Bella is alive and that his enemies will allow him a public trial in which he will call upon history and the Algerian people to defend him.

I would like to say one word about the manner in which this biography is conceived. I have written it in the first person singular in order to preserve the vivacity, the fire, and the occasional picturesqueness of the man who told me his life story. Naturally, this is a literary convention, and the form of the narrative is mine. This was the only way in which to introduce order, clarity and speed into what was, of necessity, a series of often disconnected talks. In spite of having taken liberties with both style and composition, I must emphasize the fact that I have nevertheless faithfully preserved the character of my subject. If he is alive, which I doubt, and if he ever reads this book, I have no fear that he will disown my story. If he is dead, several copies of the tape-recordings of our interviews, housed in a safe place, remain to bear witness to my good faith.

I wrote this preface a few weeks after the fall of President Ben Bella, at a moment when the Boumedienne government was maintaining total silence as to his fate. It should be noted that the government refused to allow Ben Bella to be seen by Marshal Amer, whom President Nasser had sent specially from Cairo with this object in view. At the same time some French lawyers had met with a categoric refusal when they asked not even to see Ben Bella, but to obtain from him a short tape-recorded statement reassuring them of his well-being. Under these circumstances it was natural to fear, in spite of repeated assurances from the Boumedienne government, that the conspirators had put an end to the life of the elected President of the Algerian Republic. These fears however were without foundation; that is at least, if one can believe the evidence provided by Ben Bella's family. Ahmed Ben Bella's mother saw her son on two or three occasions during 1966, and she was able to testify that when she saw him he was in good health and had been well treated. To challenge such evidence it would have to be assumed that the present powers had intimidated a poor old woman of eighty-five. This is a Machiavellian manœuvre of which I prefer to think them incapable.

I must add that, neither in foreign nor in internal politics, has the Boumedienne government initiated that reaction which one feared, and which certain of its allies expected. The Algerian Revolution has been weakened by the removal of its most renowned leader but its achievements, although constantly threatened, have not been taken away from the Algerian people.

The fact remains, nevertheless, that the proceedings against President Ben Bella which were announced with much commotion by the conspirators on the day after the 19th of June, have never been instituted; no charge has been made against the revolutionary leader.

This is one of the striking characteristics of the Boumedienne régime; its opponents are arrested without warrant and taken to a place where they are tortured, sometimes in order to extract information, at other times completely gratuitously. After this they are kept in prison for an unspecified period, sometimes in solitary confinement, at other times in communication with their families. It sometimes happens that in the end they are set free, then arrested and tortured all over again and finally liberated a second time. But during the course of all these completely arbitrary operations, no charge is made against them and no judge is called upon to pronounce on the 'offence' which they have committed. Nevertheless, at the beginning of 1966 some students did come up for trial and the judges, after acquitting them, ordered them to be discharged. To everyone's amazement, they were never set free.

It may seem extraordinary that Algeria should have set up for herself institutions which her present rulers do not dream of respecting for a moment. The elected President is in prison for an indefinite period: Parliament does not meet and no longer makes laws. The legislature is completely subjected to the executive power, which is itself controlled by the Army. The Army seized the state by force: since then it has never tried to persuade the citizens to endorse the initiative which it took, either by vote or by referendum.

ROBERT MERLE

7th January 1967

1

Marnia

I was born on the 25th December 1918 at Marnia, a small market town in the Oran district, quite close to the Moroccan frontier. My father was a *fellah*[1] and owned a small property of about seventy acres, a mile outside Marnia. But the soil was poor and there was no water supply, so my father's main source of income was the small business he ran in Marnia, where we lived.

I had four brothers. Omar, the eldest fought in the 1914–18 war in the Algerian infantry. He was seriously wounded in action and repatriated to Tlemcen, where he died as a result of his injuries. My second brother, Abdelkader, was known to us by his pet name of Kouider: he died of disease at Marnia. My third brother was called Rahal. At the outbreak of World War II, he was working in Northern France, where he had married. But in 1940 he disappeared, and all efforts to trace him were in vain. I think that he must have been killed during the evacuation.

My fourth brother was called Ouassini, after a famous *marabout*[2] of the Marnia region, Sidi Mohammed Ouassini. In 1939 he was called up by the French army; he developed tuberculosis and died in the same year. My father also died in 1939, at Marnia.

I am therefore the only survivor among the men of my

[1] Tr. note: Arabic for peasant. Plural: *fellaheen.*
[2] Tr. note: a Moslem hermit or monk.

family; but I still have my two sisters. The youngest, Hiba, is married to an *imam*,[1] Sheikh Mimoun. When I joined the secret revolutionary movement the French authorities arrested him and put him in prison, where he remained for fourteen years.

My mother is still alive; she is very old and she cannot exactly remember her age. At the end of the nineteenth century the civil status in Algeria, at any rate for the 'natives', had been somewhat neglected. The last time my mother came to see me here in the Villa Joly I said to her: "Let's see, now, mother—try and remember." "Listen, my son, I'm pretty sure I was eleven when Moulay Hassan, Mohammed V's father, died." Living as we did at Marnia, so near the frontier, everything that happened in Morocco concerned us closely. So, if her memory is correct, my mother is eighty-six.

At Marnia, during my childhood, I did not notice the difference between Frenchmen and Algerians, as much as I was to do later at Tlemcen. There was only a handful of Europeans, most of them *colons*.[2] There were a great many Jews, and the three communities lived peacefully together. For instance, the Jews, Frenchmen and Algerians of Marnia together composed the football team, and this team spirit did much to strengthen our friendship.

As far as I can remember, there was no discrimination at my school in Marnia, and I have the most affectionate memories of the two school-mistresses who taught me to read and write French. They were admirable women, whose lives were devoted to teaching. One of them came from Corsica and was called Antonini, but I cannot recall the name of the other one. I believe that they both

[1] Tr. note: the officiating priest of a mosque.
[2] Tr. note: French settlers in Algeria.

ABOVE The Casbah   BELOW Children in the upper storey of an
Algerian house (*Radio Times Hulton Picture Library*)

Primitive cooking methods (*Radio Times Hulton Picture Library*)

stayed on in the Oran district after the declaration of Independence.

The headmaster of our primary school frightened us terribly; his frown alone was enough to make us go through the floor. As he had a very large beard, it seemed quite natural to us that he should be called Barbin, and we could not imagine that he had been born without a beard, or that his father was clean-shaven or merely mustachioed. This formidable man was a strict disciplinarian; but he was also kindness itself and treated his pupils, French and Algerian alike, with scrupulous fairness.

When the moment came for the *certificat d'études*,[1] my father had to falsify my civil status and increase my age by two years, as I was too young to sit for the examination. In the villages there was no difficulty over falsifications of this kind because, as I have already said, nobody attached any importance to the civil status of the 'natives'. But this altering of a date had far-reaching consequences: I was called up for military service in 1937 instead of 1939. There is nothing so persistent as an administrative error; even now I sometimes read in biographical notes, issued officially by my own government, that I was born in 1916.

I passed my *certificat d'études* and it was decided that I should go to the nearest town for further education. A friend of my father's who lived in Tlemcen was generous enough to offer me hospitality for the time it would take to obtain my *brevet*.[1] I was twelve years old and had never been outside my own village or away from my family. It was a great adventure for me, the son of a *fellah*, to go to school in a big town.

---

[1] Tr. note: the *certificat d'études* is taken on leaving the primary school, and is roughly equivalent to our eleven-plus. The *école primaire supérieure* corresponds to our secondary school, and the *brevet* is roughly equivalent to our new Certificate of Secondary Education.

My joy did not last long. For in Tlemcen, relations between the several communities did not have the superficial good-heartedness which was to be found in the villages, and which concealed the true state of affairs. At Tlemcen, the gulf between the French world and the Algerian world was obvious. Discrimination hit you in the face, even at school. At Tlemcen I felt, for the first time, that I belonged to a community which was considered inferior by the Europeans. For the first time I realized that I was a foreigner in my own country.

I think I was fourteen when, at my *école primaire supérieure*,[1] an incident occurred which made a deep impression on me. One of the teachers was called Benavidès. In spite of his Arab name of ancient Spanish origin, he was French and an excellent teacher when he did not bore us with long digressions on the religions of the world. He was, in fact, an 'adventist', and so convinced of possessing eternal truth that he tried to convert everyone, including his pupils. There was something of the Inquisitor in this descendant of the Spaniards. Faith in his own religion made him believe that all others were bad and despicable.

One day during school, he did not hesitate to go for his Moslem pupils, launching a violent attack on Islam. "Your prophet Mohammed," he shouted at the end of this diatribe, "was nothing but an impostor!"

I stood up, pale with anger. "Sir," I told him, "it's all very well for you to say that to children. We are too young and ignorant to argue with you, but you must understand that to us our religion is sacred. No, no, it is wrong of you to speak like this." I cannot remember my exact words, because I was trembling with rage—I may have been even more outspoken. Of course Benavidès

[1] Footnote as on previous page.

blew up. It was terrible. I was punished, dismissed from the class, and even threatened with expulsion. But I stuck it out, and gradually the scandal died down. And it was a double scandal, as I well knew. Firstly, for a pupil to tick off a teacher was bad enough. But for a 'native' to stand up to a European made me a thousand times more guilty.

I remember this incident because it made me feel ill for over a fortnight and left a lasting impression on me. But it was not isolated. At school and in the town, dozens of small insults reminded me every day of the discrimination against us. I made up my mind that I myself would never submit to it, and it was from that moment that, deep in my heart, I felt myself becoming a rebel.

These conflicts and tensions had a bad effect on my work, and at the end of two years at Tlemcen I was no longer the good pupil I had been at Marnia. Also, I felt very lonely in the big town away from my father and my family. And I worried because my father's friend had had a business failure and his financial situation had suddenly become precarious. In spite of this, the admirable man would not hear of my leaving, and continued to give me food and lodging. I could not eat his bread without feelings of guilt, and I was upset by seeing these good people fighting against such hardship. All this did not help my studies to progress.

I believe that what saved my morale at this time was sport. I threw myself into it with extra keenness, especially into football, which was my passion and in which I had made very rapid progress. Of course I realize today that, at that time, football became a kind of compensation for me. The world of sport was one in which there were no restrictions and where my own ability set the only limitations. When I manœuvred the ball at high

speed against the enemy, nobody asked me whether I
was European or Algerian—I either scored a goal or
I didn't, and that was that. I was responsible only to
myself for success and failure alike.

I played centre-half, and at that time centre-half got
through a great deal of action, both offensive and defen-
sive, and was always in the thick of the battle. The game
has since changed a lot, and nowadays the players are
differently deployed on the ground; but at Tlemcen as
centre-half, I was the pivot of the team. That is to say,
of the Algerian team. For at Tlemcen, unlike what happened at Marnia, segregation had even penetrated the
world of sport. There were two teams, one of Algerians,
and one of *colons*. And once a year the *colons'* team met
ours at the Grand Bassin.

To be truthful, I must admit that the *colons* nearly
always won. I believe that we were very superior to them
in tactics and technically; but they were heavier and
more athletic than us. Let's face it, they were better
fed.

It was at this period that I made contact with Nationalist groups. The *Union Nationaliste des Musulmans
nord-africains*, which in 1937 was to become the P.P.A.
(*Parti du Peuple Algérien*), had just been founded.[1] This
National Union had attracted to itself all those Algerians
who were determined that colonialism could no longer be
tolerated as a necessary evil. It consisted mainly of
ardent and dedicated young men, one of whom, Abdelkrim Baraka, initiated me. He was a year older than me,
and was studying at a *médersa*.[2] The wave of nationalism
at that time was surging through the *médersas*, with their

---

[1] By Messali Hadj. He, however, was left behind by his followers and the struggle for
Independence began and ended without him.
[2] A Moslem religious school.

hundred per cent Moslem students, with far greater force than in the French schools. Baraka came, like me, from Marnia. He was a man of boundless generosity and unselfishness, and he gave himself body and soul to the nationalist cause. This pure-minded man inspired deep friendship in me and greatly influenced my political development. Unhappily, he died before our campaign had even begun; he was carried off at the age of twenty-five in the great typhus epidemic of 1940. Later on I lost many dear friends, but no death ever affected me so deeply as that of Baraka.

In 1934 I sat for my *brevet* examination, and was not surprised to hear that I had failed. I decided not to try again. Actually, although my failure was serious from the point of view of my personal advancement, it did not really worry me very much. By then I had already made up my mind; I was certainly not going to intrigue for some comfortable job as a minor government official, and let myself sink into a cosy routine and turn my back on the vast unhappiness of my people. I felt deep down within me, without being able to express it in so many words, that this was not the life for me, and that my personal success was of no account compared with the liberation of an entire people. The situation of the friend with whom I lodged had become even more precarious, and I felt that I could not indefinitely be the extra mouth to feed. I decided to go back to Marnia. I found employment but did not definitely commit myself to anything. I helped on the farm, I worked for some time as secretary to an insurance company, and I continued my sporting activities. I put my name down for voluntary military training at Marnia, obviously not from any excess of enthusiasm, but because I felt that the experience gained would be useful to me some day.

In 1937 I was called up for military service and posted to the 141st Alpine Infantry Regiment at Marseilles.

The 141st Regiment was billeted in the St. Charles barracks, not far from the railway station of that name. The regiment was composed of French and Algerian conscripts but our officers were all metropolitan Frenchmen, and after my first contacts with them I realized that there would be no discrimination on their part. To me, it was like entering a new world. My rights as a human being were fully recognized for the first time. I cheerfully accepted military discipline, because it was applied with equal fairness to everyone.

I was placed in the non-commissioned officers' squad and, thanks to my army practice at Marnia, I was able to follow with ease. But that was not good enough for me: I wanted to excel. On thinking it over, I believe that this was my instinctive reaction to the fairness of mind of my superiors.

I soon had fresh proof of this fairness of mind. At the end of six months, the young soldiers who were following the N.C.O.'s course had to pass an examination. I learnt later that when the total marks were being added up, there were one or two raised eyebrows when the examining officers saw that an Algerian had passed top out of a class consisting mainly of Frenchmen. But these were isolated reactions, and the examiners decided that origins were of small account and that merit was the only thing which mattered. I therefore kept the top place which my marks had won for me. This was of course only fair—but it was a fairness which would have been inconceivable in Algeria.

I was made a sergeant. Both Frenchmen and Algerians came under my orders, and in my turn I applied myself

conscientiously to the principle of making no differentia-
tion between them. At the same time, I began to learn
how to give orders.

When we began to go outside our barracks, we were
delighted with our surroundings. The town of Marseilles
is very beautiful, and so is the surrounding countryside,
which I came to know well, as I made many excursions
there with my fellow N.C.O.s and later on with my
company. As for the Marseillais, I had no difficulty in
making friends among them. I found them gay and warm
and full of life. Their exuberance astonished me; it con-
trasted strangely with the apparent coldness and reserve
of the Algerians. The odd thing was that when confronted
with the Marseillais it was we Algerians who seemed like
northerners.

I ought to have been released from the army in 1939,
but the Second World War broke out, and I was kept
with the colours and posted to an anti-aircraft battery
at Cap Janet. At Marseilles the phoney war seemed
strangely like peace, and the football matches are what
I remember best. I had become a good centre-half and,
with my friend Neckkache, I played for the excellent
Château-Gombert club, whose president was Monsieur
Ménier. I only stayed there a short time and was then
transferred to the Olympique club of Marseilles, where
I played for a whole year.

Since joining the army, I had often wondered how I
would behave in the face of danger. The bombing of
Marseilles in June 1940 provided me with an answer.
The attack was rapid and terrible. Our A.A. guns were
lined up along the harbour jetty. On a clear, bright
morning the German Stukas dived out of the sky with
a deafening whine, attacking our guns and the ships
anchored in the harbour at the same time. Several ships

were sunk in a few minutes and the jetty was badly damaged. I was the only one to remain with my gun. My men, who were mostly young soldiers, had fled, terrified by the explosions and the screaming noise of the Stukas.

That evening I had to decide what to do. I could not take back the men who had failed me in action, so I obtained permission from my officers to recruit some men myself. I chose some Corsican reservists who had recently joined the unit, and who had impressed me by their behaviour.

I could only congratulate myself on my choice. The Stukas came back the next day in wave after wave, the attack lasting for over an hour. But the Corsicans stood firm under fire, and we managed to shoot down some enemy planes. After this attack, I was mentioned in despatches and was awarded the *croix de guerre*. A few days later our colonel pinned the order on to my uniform and, as I stood at attention in front of him, I had a strange feeling of unreality. I was wearing the uniform of the French army, receiving a French decoration, and yet I did not feel myself to be a Frenchman. I certainly had no qualms at fighting for France; her war was a just one, because it was war against Fascism, and I had a good idea of what Fascism meant. As well as this, the officers and men of the 141st Regiment were all my friends. My friends, but not my brothers. When I was in their midst, in spite of their friendliness, I felt with all my heart that I was an Arab. My people were not here, but on the other side of the sea; ten million of them, poor and despised, waiting silently for the day of their liberation.

I was demobilized in 1940 and I was at once invited

to stay on in Marseilles as a professional footballer.
Financially, it was a tempting offer and I knew that I
would not have to fear any discrimination in the world
of sport. I also knew that on my return colonial Algeria
could only offer me unemployment, misery, and con-
tempt. I decided, nevertheless, to go back. As I have
already said, I felt that it was impossible for me to live
anywhere except in my own country, and that it would
be wrong to escape from the common fate of my people
through a piece of personal good fortune.

I came back to Marnia with my sergeant's stripes and
my *croix de guerre* as my only luggage—and they did not
get me a job. The situation at home was appalling. The
defeat and occupation of France had brought shortages
and high prices of foodstuffs to Algeria. For the 'natives',
who even in peacetime had had very little to spend, the
consequences were disastrous. Poverty had turned into
destitution, and destitution into utter misery. Epidemics
had added to the ravages of starvation, as is always the
case when malnutrition takes hold of large masses of
human beings. In a few years, hundreds of thousands of
people died of typhus, amongst them the dearest and
most noble of my friends, Abdelkrim Baraka.

When I got back to Marnia, I found my brother
Kouider desperately ill, and he died shortly afterwards.
War and disease had indeed struck deathly blows at my
dear ones! Omar, Rahal, Ouassini and Kouider—all my
brothers were dead. My father had also died.

My father's farm had been abandoned, so I decided to
take it in hand again. I made up my mind to increase
the arable area by removing the stones from the marginal
land. This is enormously hard work. One begins by
roughly ploughing the land, and then from this super-
ficially tilled surface one removes the stones by hand,

one by one, using them to build up low walls along the edges of the fields. The amount of land reclaimed in a day is very small, as the stones are unending. Some of them are very heavy, and from handling them not only the palms of one's hands but even the tips of one's fingers become hard and calloused. At night, with my body feeling stiff and heavy from fatigue, I would fall asleep in a second. I plunged into sleep like a stone dropping into a pool. My dreams were always of stones, and more stones, which I was continually pulling out of the earth and building into walls. The work was endless. I could have gone on for the rest of my life without ever getting to the end of my seventy acres. But at least it taught me patience, and how to go steadily on, day after day, with whatever work I had undertaken to do.

Algeria was under the Pétain régime, and agitators circulated among the people, trying to revive ancient prejudices and rouse them to massacre the Jews. But the people were on their guard against provocation, and official propaganda met with total apathy. Besides, the Algerians had quite enough problems of their own; poverty and misery were increasing from one month to the next.

I had raised a football team at Marnia, and my left wing was a Jew called Roger Benamou. It is hardly possible to believe the pressure which was put on me by the local authorities between 1940 and 1943, to make me throw him out of my team. They even went so far as to threaten me with prison for disobeying their 'suggestions'. But I utterly refused to practise odious racial discrimination against one of my good friends, remembering how often I myself had been the victim of that discrimination. Roger Benamou continued to play with my team throughout the Vichy régime. Later on, during

the Algerian war, he in turn supported us with his liberal
views. His reward was an O.A.S. plastic bomb, from
which he barely escaped with his life. After Independence
he stayed on in our country, and I had the great pleasure
of a visit from him a few months ago. He is now a solicitor
in Oran.

I persevered with my stone clearing, exhausted but
determined. For although it is hard work it is also inspir-
ing, and there is beauty in the idea of transforming even
a minute portion of the earth's surface into fertile, pro-
ductive soil. I also planted crops, especially almond trees.
At that time, knowing that war would again snatch me
up, I had no certainty that I would ever be able to
harvest a single one of my almonds. But it mattered little
to me. Other people would harvest them, and would
enjoy the beauty of the blossom before tasting the fruit.

I saw my almond trees again a few months ago, after
more than twenty years had passed. I knew that my
little house on the hillside had been destroyed. But it was
not for my house that I had come back to Marnia, but
for my almond trees, and they are still there. Or at least
nearly all of them are—a few have died. Today, I have
no idea who harvests their fruit; but when I saw them
again, looking so tall and strong after so many years, I
recaptured the deep joy which I had experienced when
I planted them.

2

The Italian Campaign

The occupation of North Africa by the Allies clearly indicated that reserves would be mobilized. I was recalled during the summer of 1943, and posted to the 6th Algerian Infantry Regiment at Tlemcen. What a contrast to the 141st Regiment at Marseilles! The discrimination practised between Algerians and Frenchmen in the ranks was flagrant. There were two completely separate officers' messes, and two separate sergeants' messes. Our plates were not allowed to fraternize with the plates of Frenchmen of the same rank. We were not allowed to touch glasses with them, even though their glasses were filled with wine and ours with water. I will not dwell on the awkwardness and the humiliations which were the result of this segregation.

The Algerians were becoming more and more resentful of this discrimination. To all people living under colonial rule, the year 1940 had burst like a clap of thunder. The course of history had broken loose from its traditional boundaries and was gathering speed. Frontiers had been overrun, states were disintegrating, everything was chaotic. We felt that Algeria could not stand aside from the great upheavals of the century. We had the impression of waking from a deep sleep, and of half steadying ourselves with one hand on the ground, on that ground which had belonged to our forefathers.

In the 6th Infantry, a movement against segregation,

of which I was the chief organizer, had begun to take place in the Algerian ranks. There was not much that we could do; but even in our restricted situation it meant a great deal to our dignity to be able to start the fight by insisting on our rights. At any rate, my superiors had no doubts as to the part I played in this matter, and a few months later I was transferred, without a word of explanation, to the 5th Moroccan Infantry Regiment. It was a clever move. I found myself, the only Algerian among Moroccans, with old professional soldiers who were strangers to any kind of ideology, and as good as married to their regiment.

As well they might be; they were well treated there. I found that the spirit of the 5th Moroccans was very different to that of the 6th Algerians. The officers were all Metropolitan Frenchmen, and the relations between the French and the Moroccans were excellent. I was placed in the company of Captain de Villaucourt. He won me over from the first moment. He was completely straight and devoid of pettiness, kind in his relations with the men, and courageous in action. As soon as I joined the regiment he sent for me, and spoke to me very frankly. He knew what my ideas were, and he respected them; but, he told me, I would be wasting my time trying to propagate them among the Moroccans. Moreover, we were going to fight; he knew that I was anti-fascist and that the struggle against Nazi Germany meant something to me. Could we not forget our differences in the fight against a common enemy? This made sense to me, and without any hesitation I promised Captain de Villaucourt not to stir up the men. He then placed me in the company of Sergeant-Major Alfonsi, where I took charge of a unit. Alfonsi was a Corsican and a strict disciplinarian in his professional duties; but he loved the Moroccans and they returned his affection a hundred-fold. Our relationship was excellent from the first day.

Ramadan began shortly after my arrival in the barracks. To my great surprise, quite a number of the Moroccans hardly kept the fast. They, in turn, were surprised to see me fasting as they looked on the Algerians, because they spoke French, as being more westernized than themselves. It saddened me that these fine men should have strayed from Islam. Although I cannot describe myself as a 'pillar of the mosque', I am a believer and I respect the precepts of my faith. I do not drink alcohol or eat ham. I must admit, however, that although I am a non-smoker, it is for reasons of health as it affects sport, rather than for strictly religious ones.

The Moroccans seemed to me at first contact to be on their guard and rather secretive, but they soon opened up and then I found them very attractive. They were all old hands. Even the 'novices' in the 5th Moroccans had already done six years service! And as for the *soldats de première classe*[1]—a much-prized distinction among the men—they all had from ten to twelve years seniority. This long period they had spent together explained the spirit of unity, almost of family affection, which prevailed. During the hard Italian campaign, the one thing which they hated (unlike most troops) was to be sent to a hospital at the rear when they were wounded. No sooner were they on their feet again than they would refuse all convalescent leave, their one idea being to rejoin their own group in the front line.

In order to avoid confusion through the absence of conventional surnames, the men were known by their army numbers. From habit, they called each other by these numbers, which were very often the only words of

---

[1] Tr. note: this distinction has no equivalent in the British army.

French which they knew. I remember a wonderful soldier, Corporal Thirty-nine. For months I had called him Thirty-nine, without giving it any further thought. After I returned to North Africa I had a letter from Captain de Villaucourt telling me of his death, and I thought for the first time how strange it was not to know his name. Captain de Villaucourt probably did not know it either, as he wrote: "Poor Thirty-nine has been killed." As I read his letter, tears came to my eyes. Poor Thirty-nine would be Thirty-nine for all eternity, and for the first time I felt ashamed that I did not know his name.

During the Italian campaign, the better part of my free time between the fighting was spent in writing letters for my Moroccans and addressing the small parcels they sent home. They managed to save some money, as after several months in the front line their modest pay had accumulated. As soon as they could, they would spend it on souvenirs, fancy jewellery, and lengths of material; the whole lot would then be sent home to their wives, in small parcels weighing three or four pounds. I spent many hours writing their letters, packing and re-packing their humble parcels, and when they asked me, giving them advice on their family problems. Although I was younger than any of them, they looked on me as their father because I was their chief, and because I took trouble over them. At the same time they showed their gratitude towards me in a way which did them great credit. Only the pure in heart are capable of real gratitude; an inferior man will always bear resentment towards the person who has done him a good turn.

We were on such good terms that I hardly needed to use words of command to the men, such was their readiness to anticipate my orders. They were used to very strict discipline, which they accepted because it was simple and straightforward; in return, they gave their complete devotion to a chief who treated them with affection and fairness.

The 5th Moroccans landed at Naples in December 1943 and were greeted on arrival by a Stuka raid. This did not do much damage as it took place at nightfall in bad visibility. The next day we pitched our camp in the mountains. It was the feast of Aïd-el-Kebir,[1] and with great difficulty we succeeded in finding a sheep for the traditional *méchoui*.[2] But we met with two disappointments: firstly, Italian mutton was too fat to be tasty, and secondly we had hardly started to eat it, when the order came to strike camp immediately and advance.

We took up our positions on a mountain called Montano, where we relieved an American unit. They were very pleased to see us, as the Germans, who were well dug in at the top, had made life difficult for them and their morale was as low as possible. I remember that at that time the Allied press had announced triumphantly that the Fifth Army was advancing at the rate of five kilometres a day towards the north. Unfortunately, it was not true. In the last seventy-five days the Fifth Army had not moved at all. The Germans, with consummate tactical skill, were holding four of Montano's five peaks. They had astutely relinquished the fifth peak to us, knowing full well the difficulty of supplying it. The only way of getting food and ammunition to the top of this four-thousand-foot rocky height was by the rudimentary method of hauling with ropes. In addition, there was snow and intense cold, and no-man's-land was scattered with corpses, which had been immobilized by the frost into weird attitudes. There was practically no shelter

---

[1] The feast of Aïd-el-Kebir is celebrated forty days after the end of *Ramadan*.

[2] Tr. note: the traditional roast lamb, cooked whole, which is eaten in all Moslem countries.

Ben Bella's arrest at Algiers Airport, 1956 (*Keystone Press*)

ABOVE Safety precautions during the Evian conference, March 1962
BELOW The referendum on Algeria's future, July 1962 (*Central Press*)

from the freezing wind, and it was impossible to use
tanks, aircraft, or even artillery because of our closeness
to the enemy. We were reduced to using small arms, as
in the 1914 fighting: guns, automatic rifles, machine-
guns, grenades and mortars. In a word, this was static
warfare in winter; we were almost at a standstill, the
cold froze one to the marrow, and there was pneumonia
and frost-bitten feet.

It was impossible to sleep that first night, with the
Germans prowling all round us in the dark. Their patrols
were operating all over no-man's-land, throwing grenades
and shouting insults at us, and playing on our nerves.
We soon realized, as the insults were all in English, that
the Germans thought the Americans were still there. The
Americans had hardly sent out any patrols and had not
even been able to tell us where the enemy outposts were
located. They had allowed the Germans to obtain the
advantage little by little, with continual sorties, harass-
ing tactics, grenade attacks, and this shouting of insults.

The colonel of the 5th Moroccans realized that we must
act, and ourselves organize counter patrols. This was not
easy, as the Germans had taken advantage of our predecessors' inactivity to stuff no-man's-land full of mines.
At the very first sortie a corporal was killed thirty yards
away from us. From our precarious shelter we could see
his body lying on the ground, and the sight upset the
Moroccan soldiers. It is radically against our religious
custom to leave a body without burial, because it is
thereby exposed to every defilement, and defilement en-
dangers the life hereafter. I realized that it was essential
to rescue the corporal's body, before it had time to have
an even more disastrous effect on the susceptibilities of
our men. I called for three volunteers and set off with
them to rescue the body. It took two hours to cover those

thirty yards. I walked in front and, in order to avoid the
German S-mines, I jumped from one to another of the
rocks which stuck up out of the thin covering of snow.
Thus, I made my way from stone to stone. It was not
easy, as they were often a long way apart. The three
volunteers had to follow exactly in my footsteps, mark-
ing the rocks which I had tested, in order to return the
same way.

The Germans soon became aware that things had
changed in the Montano sector and Allied Command,
who had witnessed our arrival with displeasure, began
to appreciate us. After the Tunisian campaign, the
Americans and the Italians had agreed secretly that there
would be no French troops in Italy. They had reckoned
without General de Gaulle. He was very anxious, and
understandably so, that France should take part in the
fight for the liberation of Europe. He had, therefore,
started to force the hand of the Allies by undertaking on
his own authority the re-conquest of Corsica. With the
same unshakable obstinacy he insisted on a French division landing in Italy.

Our division was not well received and, as can be
imagined, it was given the most disagreeable assign-
ments. We held a difficult front line without any possibility of being relieved or given a rest as, unlike the
Allied troops, we had no reserves. We became, so to
speak, the permanent element of the front line and I
have no hesitation in saying that we constituted its most
effective and experienced section. Having proved our use-
fulness so brilliantly in the field, we were kindly allowed
by the Allies to die alongside them in increasing numbers.
As the Italian campaign was gradually prolonged, other
French divisions were sent to the front and, needless to
say, were always placed in the forefront of the battle.

On the 12th January 1944, we passed over to the offensive at La Silva and the Germans withdrew, after launching a heavy artillery attack, in order to give themselves time to fall back and further hinder our progress. These artillery barrages are always on the same pattern: one section is mobile and the other remains static, trained on the unavoidable communication points. At these points, the shells fell thick and fast every two or three minutes. Our unit had managed to pass one of these threatened points and was already six hundred yards beyond it, when we suddenly noticed that R.S.M. Alfonsi was not with us. I found Captain de Villaucourt and asked: "Sir, have you seen Alfonsi?" "That's just it—I was looking for him." There was a silence, and I could read in his eyes that we were both thinking the same thing. "In any case," he said to me sharply, "you will do me the pleasure of remaining here. Do you understand? I order you to remain here." "Yes, sir," I said, and thought to myself at the same time "there are moments when one must know how to disobey orders."

I went off to find Alfonsi. The heaviness of the firing was unbelievable and I made slow progress. I found him stretched out within full range of the guns, seriously wounded and unconscious. I hoisted him onto my back and got him away; but instead of evacuating him back past the firing-line to our rear lines, I took him forward to our front line. Villaucourt, who was both furious and pleased at the same time, gave me the wigging which was my due. "And now," he said, "all you have to do is to take him back to the other side of the firing-line to our first-aid post." This I did, but this time with two private soldiers to help me. Alfonsi was still motionless and unconscious. He recovered, but he was too badly wounded to return to the front. I saw him again seven months later at the Oujda depot, still with a badly shattered arm and furious at having missed the last part of the war.

A few days later, the 20th January, if I remember rightly, we attacked at Santa Croce. It was a remarkably tough battle at a height of over five thousand feet, the same position changing hands several times. The enemy line and the Allied line were so close together that in the end we could hardly distinguish between the Germans and our own men. To add to the confusion, the summit of the mountain was wreathed in mist. In trying to contact my neighbouring unit, I lost myself in the mist and landed up less than thirty feet from the Germans. Luckily I heard one of them talking, so I stopped, and doubled back on my tracks. I had no wish to end the war as a prisoner.

Captain de Villaucourt was wounded in the leg, and it took no less than five men to carry him down to the hollow where Alfonsi had been hit, and from there to the first-aid post. Although the captain was less seriously wounded than Alfonsi, he was in great pain from the jolts which we were inflicting on him. But he did not once complain, nor did he at any time lose consciousness.

In my opinion, German morale was beginning to weaken at Santa Croce. At Montano and La Silva we had taken a few prisoners, but at Santa Croce, for the first time since the beginning of the Italian campaign, whole units surrendered. I do not know how to explain this phenomenon, unless it could be that in static warfare, when two forces are face to face for rather a long time, one side in the end inevitably gains the upper hand by showing more spirit of initiative and enterprise. You can feel the moment when the enemy is suddenly going to give in, not because you are hitting harder, but because he senses your superiority.

Nevertheless, the unit which faced us was a good one. They were Panzer troops who, because of the nature of the ground, had to fight without their tanks and were therefore all the more deserving of merit. Their setback was, in fact, only temporary, and they recovered a short distance beyond Santa Croce. Our advance was halted at an admirably chosen and well-organized point: Cassino.

Once again we came to a standstill. Our unit had lost a fair number of men and some of its N.C.O.s, and it was now commanded by an Alsatian sub-lieutenant, called Z. He showed little courage in action, and great meanness out of it. I had already noticed this more than once; the best officers are invariably those who behave well in action. Conduct under fire is the surest test of the attitude of an officer towards his men. A coward under fire will also be cowardly in human relationships, without generosity, fairness, or loyalty. Z. was one of these. It so happened that during one attack he was 'absent': when all danger had passed and quiet had returned, he was the first to start giving orders, flaunting his rank and his rights. Unfortunately, I had more contact with him than I wished, as I had to work alongside him as his company sergeant-major.

The situation worsened when parcels began to arrive for the French division in Italy, sent by French people living in North America, for the New Year's Day festivities. Some block-headed officer, sitting snug and warm in his office behind the lines, had thought up an army order whereby all parcels for the front line were to be distributed as follows: one parcel for each Frenchman, and one to be shared between three Moroccans. As soon as I knew of this order, I went to Z. and pointed out to him with some force the odious nature of such discrimination. He at once took a haughty line, saying that he approved of the order and intended to enforce it. I blew up, and gave him some very rough words. I reminded him, amongst other things, of his cowardice in action, and I left without saluting him, blind with rage.

The order about the parcels was particularly ill-advised as there existed such remarkably good relations between the French and the Moroccans in the front line. They both felt that they were equal in face of the threat of death: if enemy fire made no distinctions, neither did their friendship. The fact that Z. could not understand this shows how completely he lacked humanity. My blowing-up had been wasted on him; the only thing he remembered was the fact that a sergeant had shown disrespect. So he wrote a long report to the commanding officer: I was an 'agitator', and certainly did not deserve the *médaille militaire*[1] for which I had been recommended.

A few days later, an officer came to tell me that Captain de Villaucourt had asked me to go and see him in hospital. I got a jeep and drove off at once; it was a little journey of two hundred and fifty miles, which helped to cool my rage. The captain was very much better, and I lost no time in telling him of the incident. He assured me that I was in the right and sent me back to my unit feeling much calmer. A week later, sublieutenant Z. got the sack. He had been transferred to the burial squad, no longer to fight, but to bury those who had died in battle. His unfavourable report on me was buried too.

At any rate the incident was not entirely useless; it

---

[1] Tr. note: one of the highest decorations in the French army, which has been compared with the V.C.

succeeded in uniting almost all the N.C.O.s against the infamous army order, and the distribution of the parcels from America was carried out fairly among the troops.

I did not touch my parcel; I could never eat American corned beef, canned beans, jams and jellies. All this artificial, tasteless tinned stuff did not suit me. I had decided to live on bread and honey, and I did very well on it throughout the campaign. I always carried two flasks fastened to my belt, one filled with water or coffee, and the other with honey. The honey was acquired for me by my orderly, though I hesitate to call him by this name. I should say, rather, that he was my friend. He was a young *Chleuh*[1] of barely nineteen, tall and strong and very tough. He could talk no French, and hardly any Arabic. But he had one invaluable gift: wherever he went, he always managed to ferret out some beehives. I have seen him, apparently unaffected by bee-stings, imperturbably removing the honey from the hives. Thanks to him, I never once went without my favourite food throughout the whole Italian campaign.

At the beginning of these operations, I was armed with an American Garand gun. It was accurate, but enormously heavy, so I soon replaced it with a carbine; this was also of American manufacture and its only merit was lightness, as a speck of dust would cause it to jam. I found it essential not to overload myself, as I had to move about a great deal when commanding my section, choosing the positions of outposts and establishing liaisons. I also carried a pistol at my belt, of which I shall speak later.

This was therefore my equipment during the Italian campaign: two weapons and two flasks, the wherewithal to fight and the means of survival. My life was a hard

[1] Tr. note: a North African tribesman, found only in Morocco.

one, and a full one. I was fighting for a just cause, and I believe that I was happy. Or at least I would have been, if the thought of unhappy Algeria had ever left me for a moment.

The period of static warfare at Cassino was for me the most trying part of the campaign. Living in snow and mud and being constantly pounded by enemy artillery was most disagreeable. We were reduced to a third of our original number, and that third had suffered great hardship. Wounds, pneumonia and frost-bite continued to take their toll. I was the only one who had not once been evacuated, but I had contracted sciatica from sleeping out in the snow, and I was very lame. Captain de Villaucourt had rejoined us, only to be wounded once more; as he left for hospital, he asked me to hold out until he could get back again. He did not want the company to disintegrate. Men with no battle experience were being sent out as replacements, and we had to take them in hand under appalling conditions, which was not easy.

Captain de Villaucourt came out of hospital just in time for the big offensive which was being mounted. We attacked Cassino at eleven o'clock at night, to cut off the German retreat on the left. Our command had discovered the Germans' weak point: they did not like night attacks. Neither did we, but the surprise element and the ensuing panic among the enemy ranks were well worth the effort involved.

Cassino fell. The offensive continued and we penetrated without being halted. It was the best part of the campaign. But the Germans still had plenty in store for us. We were approaching Rome, and coming down into the plain one night our troops began to find that they were meeting with very weak resistance. We ought perhaps to have been more wary, but after months of inactivity we

ABOVE Ben Bella's visit to Nasser, April 1962—Egyptian children present bouquets (*Keystone Press*)   BELOW The *Gouvernement Provisoire* in Rabat—Ben Bella is talking to King Moulay Hassan II of Morocco (*London Express News and Feature Service*)

Tumultuous scenes of welcome on Ben Bella's arrival in Algiers
(*London Express News and Feature Service*)

were drunk with the speed of our advance. At daybreak we found ourselves face to face with the Panzers. These huge tanks, suddenly roaring over the top of a rise and opening fire on our ranks almost point-blank with a burst of shells, had the most terrifying effect on us.

There was no shelter except from the craters made by the exploding shells. I marked down one of these craters, waited for a lull, took an enormous leap—and landed on top of Captain de Villaucourt, who had got there first. Our amazement lasted for a second, and then we both collapsed with uncontrollable laughter. On looking back, I can only think that our laughter was the instantaneous reaction from fear. In the midst of that hell we were at least both of us still alive.

Our company had clearly stopped fighting, as we could only hear a few bursts of rifle fire. The captain said to me, "Go out in front and see what's happening. Something must have gone wrong." I went, and found one of the platoon commanders, a sub-lieutenant from Catalonia. He said to me: "It's very serious—the men have retreated, leaving their machine-guns behind them." "All three machine-guns?" I asked. He nodded his head, and I looked at him, horror-stricken. What would happen to the company without its machine-guns? I said: "I am going to see," and I started to crawl. Our firing positions were only about fifty to a hundred feet away from where the Panzers had halted. I was sweating profusely as, all alone, I drew near to what was left of the firing positions and was now a part of no-man's-land, pitted with shell craters. Luckily nobody spotted me. One by one, I found the machine-guns and brought them back to our lines. As I had to crawl most of the way, I could only bring back one at a time, and I had to make three separate journeys.

3

It was a great relief to see the nice kind face of the Catalonian sub-lieutenant once more. We agreed to keep the incident quiet in order to avoid having to court-martial the men for abandoning their arms. The Panzer attack had been so terrible, and so many of our men had been killed, that we felt they had had some reason to panic.

I had hardly got back to the lines when a Moroccan came up to me saying: "Sergeant, your *Chleuh* is wounded, they have just taken him away." I ran to catch up, and two hundred yards away I found him on a stretcher, lying on his stomach. He had never looked so tall. "How are you feeling?" I said. "It's nothing," he answered, lifting his head and smiling. He had a horrible wound in his back, which had been ripped open by a shell right down to the bone. "Get well quickly," I said. "May Allah hear your words!" The stretcher bearers set off again, but they had hardly gone a hundred yards before they stopped. "Sergeant!" one of them called, "he wants to say something to you." I ran to him. "I thought of you," said my *Chleuh*. He rolled himself carefully on to one side, and pulled out from under him a can of honey and handed it to me. I stood beside him speechless, with the can in my hand. But the stretcher-bearers were impatient to be off again. "Come back soon," I said. "I'll be back!" And he kept his word. He recovered in record time, refused to take convalescent leave (like all of them) and came back to the front line to regain his health fighting.

At last we came to the Eternal City. Contrary to the subsequent claim of the Allies, it was the French who first entered Rome.

It was here that, for the first time, I made contact with some members of the Italian Resistance. Afterwards, they fought with us north of Siena. I would like, once and for all, to put right the false theory that the Italian is a man without courage under fire. It is completely untrue. The Italian is very subtle, not easily convinced, and very wary of propaganda; he does not go into battle blindfold. But once he has decided that the goal is desirable and worth while, he is ready to give his life. The partisans who fought at our side knew exactly what they wanted: to banish fascism from their country. Although they had not acquired the same proficiency and discipline as our men, they showed great courage in carrying out the tasks which had been assigned to them.

Shortly after the capture of Rome, I was decorated with the *médaille militaire*. Since the beginning of the campaign I had been mentioned four times in despatches. It was on the strength of these four mentions, and also on account of the machine-gun business that I was given this medal. (Much as I had wanted the machine-gun business hushed up in order to avoid penalizing the men, it had leaked out in the end.) There was a ceremonial parade, and General de Gaulle came specially to Italy to take part in it, and it was he who decorated me. Little did the great statesman know, when he pinned the medal on my uniform and gave me the accolade, that standing in front of him was the man who, eighteen years later, was to become president of the independent Republic of Algeria.

3

Return to Algeria

After Siena, the 5th Moroccans were relieved and sent into reserve in order to take part later in the invasion of France. When this happened, I obtained special leave to return to my family at Marnia. When my leave was up, I joined the depot at Oujda, where to my delight I found R.S.M. Alfonsi. "I'm not going to let you go," he said at once, "I need you to help train recruits."

It was at Oudja that rumours reached me of the events of 1945.[1] I was profoundly shocked by the fierce repressive measures which followed the rising. According to the evidence, it was quite clear that, when the war was over, colonialism was not going to cede anything to the Algerians, and that rule by fear would prevail.

I was meditating on this bitter lesson, when my chiefs suggested that I should stay on in the French army. They would send me to an officers' training college; with my good service record, I would very soon become a second lieutenant. I refused the offer, giving as my reason the fact that my family was in distress, and that I felt I must return to Marnia to look after my mother and sisters. In reality, it was the events of Constantine which made me decide to refuse. I felt as though the decision had been

[1] The rising known as the rising of Sétif had, in fact, affected several other centres in the district of North Constantine. In an apparently peaceful part of the country, this sudden, violent flare-up cost the lives of several dozen Europeans. Retaliatory measures, which were inhuman and out of all proportion, accounted for forty thousand Algerian dead.

made for me. The retaliations at Sétif had created an un-
bridgeable gulf between the two communities. I felt that
I owed it to the people of my own community to return
home, and that I must endeavour by all the means in my
power to improve their lot and rectify the injustice from
which they had suffered.

No sooner had I returned to Marnia than my compatriots asked me to put my name down on a list of can-
didates for the municipal elections. The list was not very
consistent but it was composed, for the most part, of
well-intentioned Algerians; so I agreed to join them.

The electors of the *Second Collège*![1] This delightful
euphemism was used to describe the Algerians. The
Premier Collège naturally, was composed of Europeans:
first they were, and first they intended to remain. For the
aim of this '*Deux Collèges*' system was none other than to
adjust the workings of universal suffrage. Thus, in the
whole of Algeria, ten million Algerians elected one-third
of the municipal councillors, whereas one million Europeans elected the other two-thirds. In each parish, the
elected members of the *Second Collège* (by its terms of
reference given minority representation) were reduced to
playing the part of '*Algériens de service*'; resigned and
powerless, they were passive onlookers of the administration of the *Premier Collège*. They were perpetual yes-men,
who were intended to provide the colonial system with a
semblance of democracy. I must confess to feelings of
deep scepticism when those same politicians who in-
vented this splendid institution of the two *collèges* accuse
present-day Algeria of not being sufficiently democratic.
We have attained the fundamental truth of democracy:
it is called *autogestion*. As for the other kind of democracy,

[1] Tr. note: in French electoral procedure, the word '*collège*' is used in the late Latin
sense of an electorate, cf. 'the College of Cardinals'.

with its ready-made electoral laws, its intrigues, its *Deux Collèges*, and its clever carving-up of districts, we prefer to leave that kind of democracy to these same gentlemen.

At the very first meeting of the town council of Marnia, it was clear to us that the members of the *Premier Collège*, secure in their superior numbers, had no intention of delegating any authority to the members of the *Second Collège*. It meant that we were denied even the smallest share in the administration of the little town and consequently we were unable to be of use to our electors. The members of the *Second Collège* resigned in a body, and were immediately re-elected, in a body, by the electors of the *Second Collège*. There followed a new meeting of the town council, at which we renewed our demands for the delegation of power, which met with the same refusal as before. A second mass resignation resulted, followed by further elections. In all, we returned three times to our electors.

The hostility of the *Premier Collège* towards us increased each time, particularly with regard to myself, as they considered me to be the ringleader and the toughest element. The *Premier Collège* could neither vote for nor administer the budget by itself, and although they were in the majority, they were unable to move without us. But we, the minority, only had the right to agree—and in order to disagree, we had to resign. The alternatives were, to agree to everything, or to turn everything down.

The Mayor, Monsieur Gerbaud, was fully aware of the absurdity of the situation. He was a socialist, a member of the S.F.I.O.;[1] but this brand of socialism has, I fear, unhappy associations for us Algerians. Gerbaud was a decent fellow, but in order to obtain a minimum of administrative power from this so-called socialist, it took us

[1] Tr. note: *Section Française de l'Internationale Ouvrière.*

three elections. He gave in at the third one—or rather, he thought up a plan. We wanted administrative power: all right, he would let us have it—in full measure! He was convinced, like all Europeans in Algeria, that we "didn't know how to do anything" and that we "couldn't do without them". He thought that he would overwhelm us with hard work and the weight of our responsibilities. What a blow was in store for him! We took on all the tasks he assigned to us, and they did not overwhelm us at all.

I managed to get myself put in charge of food supplies and rationing, which were both at that time an essential part of the machinery of municipal administration, as everything was still rationed. Rationing caused no hardship to the rich, as anything could be had for money. But the poor only had the coupons on their ration-cards, without which they could get nothing. Great numbers of penniless *fellaheen* had drifted into the towns from the fields, hoping for crusts of bread, a few dates, or a handful of semolina. When they found that there was nowhere to sleep in Marnia, they camped out in caves along the banks of the river, in a state of indescribable destitution. Along with starvation, typhus came to ravage the undernourished masses. In a small town like Marnia, with under ten thousand inhabitants, around ten people a day were carried off. As for the people who died in the caves, we had no idea of their numbers. Without any hesitation, I signed thousands of ration-cards which I ought not to have signed for these wretched people. I did not care what the regulations were: those hungry mouths had to be fed.

I worked from morning till night, visiting people and discussing their problems, which Heaven knows were unending. I was active, and I felt I was being useful. It was to me a remarkably stimulating period; I was in excellent physical shape and felt full of drive. It was as though I was still living on the moral stimulus of Cassino. At first there were endless difficulties with the Mayor but, as I have said before, he was a decent fellow and, through being among us and seeing us at work, he finally outgrew his prejudices, and we were able to come to terms with him. Our worries no longer came from him, but from higher up.

As well as being a town councillor, I was also a militant member of the M.T.L.D.[1] The way in which I carried out my daily tasks on behalf of my fellow-citizens of Marnia had, in a few months, attracted new supporters to my side, and had turned Marnia into a party headquarters. The chief colonial administrator and his henchmen, the *bachagas*[2] and the *caïds*,[3] could not forgive me for this.

One day my brother-in-law, who lived in Marnia, came to see me, looking worried. "Ahmed," he said to me, "So-and-So has moved into your farm and is claiming that it belongs to him." "I will go and fling him out," I answered. "Be careful," my brother-in-law replied, raising his right hand in warning, "I have a feeling that this is a trap. The man himself is not particularly dangerous, because he is a legless cripple. But his cousins are brigands, real killers who have just got back from Cayenne. May Allah protect you!"

I went to see the cripple, who was indeed in possession of my house. He received me as though he were quite at home, with a wife on either side. He reeled off a long and complicated story which was meant to prove that my

---

[1] *Mouvement pour le Triomphe des Libertés Démocratiques.*
[2] Tr. note: rulers over small districts, who were part and parcel of the French colonialist system.
[3] Tr. note: civil judges in Arab countries.

farm really belonged to him. Needless to say, he had not
even the shadow of documentary proof. But unfortunately, neither had I anything in writing to protect my
rights, as land that had already belonged to native families before the conquest of Algeria never carried any title-
deeds. Property was owned by right of long occupation;
my land was mine because my father had cultivated it,
and he had inherited it from his father, and so on. There
was endless litigation, as it was always easy for a dis-
honest man to pretend that his great-grandfather had
been robbed of his land by your great-grandfather in a
squabble over inheritance. The colonial administration
made the most of these quarrels, sometimes even creating
them in order to favour those whom they considered to be
'good natives' against the 'bad natives'.

It seemed to me, on thinking it over, that I had been
placed in the latter category. The cripple, although
scared to death of me, showed considerable determina-
tion, which I felt sure was backed up by someone other
than his cousins from Cayenne.

The more I listened to him, the more I was convinced
that my brother-in-law was right, and that the whole
business had been rigged by the administration. If I gave
in, I would be dispossessed of my rights and discredited
in the eyes of my fellow-citizens. If I resorted to violence,
the cousins were there to eliminate me physically. They
would be tried as a matter of form, but the murder of a
'native' by another 'native' was of no importance. Ten
witnesses would be found who would swear great oaths
that the murderer had acted in self-defence.

I thought of all this as I listened to the cripple, and all
at once I recovered my composure. It is strange that I
cannot remember the cripple's name, but I can still see
his face, which showed terror and arrogance at the same

time. His two wives stood behind him, looking more dead
than alive, as my talk with him had been loud and angry,
especially at the beginning. There was a silence. I looked
at the man and said: "Just you wait—I'll see about
you!" And I turned on my heels. I remember vaguely
wondering, as I slammed the door behind me, how it was
that he, a legless cripple, should need two wives!

I tried by every possible legal means to recover my
property, but I was up against a brick wall. My final step
was to ask for an interview with the administrator. The
way in which he received me left me devoid of hope: he
was triumphant. His eyes sparkled with malice and he
never once dropped his sarcasm, even when I reminded
him of my war record. Apparently it all meant nothing
to him, neither my *croix de guerre*, nor my mentions in
despatches, nor my *médaille militaire*. All that mattered
to him was my 'attitude' at Marnia, and the progress of
the M.T.L.D. I got up to go, and said to him: "Tell me,
monsieur l'administrateur, what exactly are you driving
at?" He answered in the same ironic voice: "You will
see all right," and then added: "You think you're pretty
smart, Ben Bella, but we will show you that we are even
smarter than you." As I left, I realized that I had lost
the farm.

When I returned to Marnia, on thinking over the situation, I decided to attack. One morning I drove an empty
lorry over to the farm. Pistol in hand, I walked up to the
house, opened the door, and said to the cripple in a loud
voice: "I give you ten minutes to clear out. Take your
rags and your wives and go." He was not alone, but had
with him one of the cousins from Cayenne. But my attack
had taken them by surprise, and they could do nothing.
Everything went off in the most exemplary manner. The
clothes, the household chattels, the two wives, the cripple

and his cousin were piled into the back of the lorry and the driver drove off, leaving me in possession.

But I knew that this all too easy victory was sure to lead to a counter-attack: and it came, three days later. I was asleep in my house when, in the middle of the night, I was woken by a colossal din. Somebody was hurling stones at my shutters. I did not move. The stones continued, accompanied by shouted insults. Still I did not move. The stones and the insults went on all night.

Their plan was obvious: one of them was throwing stones while the other lay in ambush, watching my door and ready to shoot if I should appear, exasperated, on the threshold.

I waited for daylight to make my getaway. I got my gun ready; it was a long-barrelled P.38 revolver, with a very accurate range of over two hundred yards. When I turned the cripple out of my house I carried a much smaller gun in my hand, a 6·35, and the cousins must have thought that it was the only one I possessed. Consequently, they had taken up their positions only about sixty-five yards from my house, bringing it comfortably within range of their breach-loading rifles. They fancied themselves to be out of range of the gun which they believed me to be using, and they were quite sure that when I emerged they would be safe from my bullets, whereas I would be in full receipt of theirs. It will be seen that these killers had had a certain amount of experience in the art of ambushing.

Meanwhile, the stones and the insults continued. I sat on a chair in the dark, silent and still, the P.38 in my hand. The long wait was very trying for me, but having been through Cassino, I knew that it was just as bad for them.

At daybreak I passed over to the attack. I suddenly

opened the door, jumped out and threw myself on the
ground. Two shots rang out over my head: they missed
me, and showed me the position of the rifles. I sprang up,
ran in their direction, let off a full round, and once again
flung myself down. They must have been horribly surprised by this hail of bullets, thinking as they did, that I
was only armed with a 6·35 pistol. I slipped a fresh round
into my gun, jumped forward again, fired, then again fell
flat on the ground. There were shouts and the sound of
running feet, and I knew that they had fled. I ran after
them, as I did not want to give them time to re-load
their rifles. But they ran without any thought of returning. I saw some blood on a scrub bush, so I knew that
I must have hit one of them. I had to stop for breath;
I was recovering from a bout of malaria, and was out of
condition and unable to run any further.

I set off for the town to let my family and friends know
that I was all right. On the way, I met the *caïd* coming
towards me. He was a fat hypocrite, and he gave me an
oily smile from afar. He bade me good morning and asked
me what had happened, stealing furtive and rather
alarmed glances at the P.38, which was still in my hand.
The fact that he had come to meet me, together with his
saintly expression and his guarded questions, convinced
me that it was he who had organized the whole thing,
with the connivance of the administrator. I told him so
in the harshest terms. I was still hot from the fight, and
the names 'traitor' and 'hireling' were about the nicest
things I called him. He kept on looking at my gun, feeling
himself to be very much alone with me on that road. He
did not even try to deny anything, but stood without
daring to look up, pale, with shaking cheeks and all his
dignity gone, while I blasted him.

On my way back to Marnia I thought to myself that,

although I had won, my victory was only a Pyrrhic one. The fact that I had wounded someone was enough to get me arrested and imprisoned: so I decided to leave at once. By leaving Marnia I would lose my inheritance, but I would keep my liberty, which was far more precious to me. I needed to be free in order to serve my party and the cause of Independence.

I went to Algiers, and changed my name. This was in 1947, and from that date onwards I became a clandestine fighter, and remained one until the day of my arrest.

Owing to the pressure of events, a crisis had blown up in the M.T.L.D.; a split had widened between the leaders of the party and its more determined fighting members. The latter had obliged the leaders to form a secret organization, of which I became the chief. We called it the *Organisation Spéciale*. It ended by becoming a party within a party, so different were its aims and its mentality to those of Messali. He, in fact, was becoming more and more constitutional, and believed that thanks to the elections the situation would evolve and that we would eventually be able to make ourselves heard and gradually obtain more concessions from the colonial administration. Like all the young fighters of the *Organisation Spéciale*, I could only believe that his view was an illusion. We were anxious to take action, as the events of Sétif had convinced us that, sooner or later, it would be a question of using force, and that we must prepare ourselves for this.

The rigged elections of 1948, organized by the 'socialist' Naegelen, emphatically confirmed our point of view. No parody of the democratic voting system has ever been conducted with such cynicism. The policy of nagging which followed served to enlighten us. It was as though the colonial administration bore the Algerians a grudge for having won the pure formality of the right to vote, and for having put it to all the trouble of having had to fake the election results. Every meanness which could be thought up by a colonial bureaucrat was practised against my brother Algerians. The Moorish cafés were closed down. Peasants were fined for riding their donkeys on the wrong side of the road. These small irritations accumulated the whole time, and created an atmosphere of hate. It was obvious that the object of these petty restrictions was to punish us for our inexcusable and tremendous 'presumption' in claiming the right to vote, even though these elections were always fixed before-hand. We were undergoing a system of punishment which in military parlance would be called 'a regaining of con-trol'. The system was brutal, as well as niggling and petty; it was intended to make the 'native' once and for all 'know his place'—and his place was the lowest in the land.

It was part of my work to go from village to village, visiting our militant supporters and persuading sympa-thizers to join our ranks. My visits were secret; I never stayed in hotels, but always with local people, and I went out very little. I discovered that peasant opinion was very similar to my own. As they did not know of the existence of the *Organisation Spéciale*, they could only judge the activities of the M.T.L.D. by the pronounce-ments of its leaders, with whom they were thoroughly disgusted. "Listen, my son," a peasant said to me one day, "do you know what happens if the administration finds out that one of us is a member of the M.T.L.D.? They send the police to drag him out of his house and beat and humiliate him in front of his wife; then they fling him into prison without trial. When he comes out, he is bullied by the *bachaga* and the *caïd*. That is the system. We are crushed, oppressed, and ground underfoot. And after all this, the party talks to us of elections! Of what use are elections? To parade about among the French? To take part in their municipal councils, their assemblies, their political meetings? What would all this lead us to? To some minor progress, perhaps in a hundred years' time. But in a hundred years' time we will all be dead. No, my son, we don't want to hear any more about elections. What we want now is—guns."

We heard this kind of talk everywhere, and we did not fail to pass it on, with vehemence, to the leaders of our party. But it was impossible to shake them out of their 'wait-and-see' policy. Their attitude can only be described as one of readiness for flight; they shirked making any necessary decisions. The thought of armed rebellion against the colonial power scared them, and the idea of a general revolt did so even more. They kept on postponing vital decisions to some future date, and taking refuge meanwhile in constitutionalism. If only the elections had been genuine, and if only the power of the elected members had been real! Faced with the massive and hopeless oppression which weighed our people down, the party's parliamentary ambitions seemed ludicrous.

The party leaders were only aware of one aspect of the alienation of the masses from the party: membership had dwindled, and subscriptions were no longer coming in. Political parties have always existed on the contributions of the poor and humble, such as the *fellaheen*, who make sacrifices to keep them going; it was these people who were now beginning to desert us in increasing numbers. I remember that at that time the finances of the M.T.L.D. had fallen so low that we sometimes had difficulty in paying our regular staff.

In 1949 the situation was so disastrous that our militant members were roused into forcing Messali and his acolytes to summon a congress. By a remarkable irony of history, the sessions of this congress took place in the region controlled by the *bachaga* Boualem. We were actually the guests of a certain Djilali, who put us up in his farm at Ezzidine. This Djilali later betrayed the party and became a police informer under the name of Khabous, but at that time he had not yet taken the road to dishonour.

About sixty delegates came from all parts of the country to the Congress. From the very first session it quickly became clear that the majority would repudiate the wait-and-see policy of Messali and his friends, who were in the minority. History repeats itself. In 1949, this minority was determined to remain 'within the law', and to immobilize the party by their constitutionalism. They were conservatives by instinct, opportunists by temperament, and sceptics *a priori*. Today, in independent Algeria I find the same people, opposing all revolutionary government reform; they have not changed, and are just as eloquent, and just as determined not to move.

The Congress of 1949 made some major decisions without the consent of these people. It decided that the party should place the major part of its funds at the disposal of the *Organisation Spéciale*. In order to make sure that this decision did not remain merely a dead letter, the Congress appointed me as chief political organizer of the party, as well as head of the *Organisation Spéciale*.

The time had come for action. Our propaganda work was being considerably hampered at this time by vagrant bands recruited by the *caïds* and *bachagas* to terrorize the districts under their control. The best-known of these gangs was run by the *bachaga* Aït Ali, in Kabylia. His men were thorough scoundrels, highway robbers who pillaged and murdered with complete impunity. These killers acted against our members in all cases where the administration did not wish to soil its hands, using the same methods which had operated against me at Marnia, which I have already exposed. The *Organisation Spéciale*, emerging strengthened and invigorated from the 1949 Congress, decided to take action against these thugs. With some difficulty, permission to neutralize them was obtained from the party leaders. This was a police operation, rough but necessary, and it did much to change the atmosphere in Algeria.

If I remember rightly, it was at this time that the *Organisation Spéciale* decided to blow up the monument which had been erected by the authorities to the memory of the Emir Abd-el-Kader. He was a national hero who had fought for fifteen years to defend the independence of Algeria against the invader, and it seemed to us sacrilegious that the colonial administration should now claim him as an ally. The operation was not entirely successful, but nevertheless our attempt helped in large measure to clarify public opinion.

The party's lack of funds continued to paralyse our movements, and the young active members of the *Organisation Spéciale* decided that, at all costs, we must escape from this situation. We did not have the same careful bourgeois scruples about money as our leaders had, because we ourselves were completely disinterested. We told them: "There is no shortage of money in Algeria: we must get it from the banks and post offices, where there is plenty. Let us be consistent: if we are prepared to stake our lives in a violent attack against the occupier of our country, we must not hesitate to plunder his safes." The leaders finally agreed to our plan in principle, with many wry faces, and after having carefully absolved themselves of all responsibility.

The plan was to raid the Oran post office. Our intelligence had been thorough, and we reckoned to lay our hands on thirty million francs, which would have filled the party's coffers in one fell swoop and allowed us to purchase arms. In actual fact the haul was very much smaller.

The raid was very carefully organized. In order to deflect suspicion from our members, we decided to disguise the attack as a hold-up by Pierrot-le-Fou, whose exploits were filling the newspapers at that time. We chose fair-haired Algerians as our men for the job, dressed them in European clothes, and told them to speak with a Paris accent.

Our subterfuge was successful. The newspapers at once detected the hand of Pierrot-le-Fou, and commented with some surprise on the fact that he had now transferred his operations to North Africa. But our luck was not destined to hold, and an unbelievable series of infinitesimal mischances began to act against us.

The raiders had used a rather worn old suitcase to remove the bank-notes and, in the hurry of getting away, part of the metal fitting had caught on something, and a minute fragment had broken off and fallen onto the carpet of the black front-wheel drive car which they were using. This fragment, although very small, was found by the police investigators and preserved as a possible piece of incriminating evidence. However, time passed, no real clues materialized, and the inquiries came to a standstill. Then one day, an officer of the criminal police department, who had been taking part in the inquiries, was transferred to the department of *Renseignements Généraux*.[1] This man was sent to search the house of one of our active members and took a fancy to a suitcase,

[1] Tr. note: the Intelligence Service of the police force.

which he decided to confiscate for his personal use. This minor act of plunder had serious results for us. When he got the suitcase home, the police officer had some difficulty in opening it: he looked at it more closely and noticed that a piece of metal was missing. Then he remembered the minute scrap of evidence which he had handled a few months earlier. He rushed off to the police station with the suitcase, where he proved that the broken fitting and the small piece of metal corresponded exactly. He realized in a flash that the Oran post office raid was no ordinary hold-up organized by Europeans, but an operation mounted by our party. Arrests and torture began from that moment and finally they got onto my trail.

The first time I was nearly arrested was in February 1950, at Algiers Central Post Office. But I succeeded in pushing my way past the police, and took to my heels. I saw that they were following me, so I took my revolver from my pocket, brandished it over my head without firing it, and never stopped running until I saw that I had outdistanced them. Doubtless discouraged by the prospect of an exchange of shots, the police gave up, and I got away.

But it was only a brief respite. A month later they caught me in my hiding-place in Algiers; I had been denounced by a traitor.

The police had discovered the existence of our organization, but in the long run they only managed to arrest a few of our militant members, or 'shock troops'. They had, however, found out enough to be able to call it a plot, and of course they flattered themselves that it had been nipped in the bud and crushed.

As was to be expected, the party leaders took fright and dissociated themselves from our attempted *coup*. At the same time they conveyed to me, and to the men who were accused with me, that the case was to proceed without publicity.

We took good care to disobey these orders because, if our action was to make any sense, we had got to justify it by loudly proclaiming the underlying political motives. In consequence, we adopted a fighting attitude from beginning to end and reversed our position from that of accused to that of accusers, turning our trial into a trial of colonialism. We even kept up our aggressive action outside the law-court; from the prison to the court and back again, we sang our national hymn in unison, and at the tops of our voices. Every means, including pressure, threats and sanctions, was used to try to stop our singing. In the end, the police, who could not silence us, had to arrange to make us inaudible. They surrounded our prison van with an army of motor-cycle outriders, who raced their engines whenever we opened our mouths. Luckily for us, they had to stop when they came to the steps of the Palais de Justice; we never missed a chance to sing our hymn when entering or leaving the court, in the presence of the magistrates.

I had not myself taken part in the Oran raid, but I had planned it. I proudly claimed my responsibility in front of the judges, and I was sentenced to eight years' imprisonment. When the gates of Blida prison closed on me and my companions, the party leaders heaved a sigh of relief. At last they were rid of the trouble-makers! Now they could give their full time to the delights, and the evils, of constitutional intrigue. Their first act was to abolish the *Organisation Spéciale*, as they thought, for ever. They then took care to disperse, isolate, and reduce to impotence all its more dynamic members. Those who had been the leaders in the Constantine area were transferred to Oran, and vice versa; the most active ones were sent to France. Valuable regular staff members were purposely left without funds. Souidani, who was later to die a hero's death in the war of liberation, was forced to earn his living as an agricultural labourer on the land of a *colon* in the Mitidja district, together with one of our fighters, Bouchaïb, who is no longer alive today.

As for myself, I was put under lock and key, not in a prison cell, but in a vast hall with sixty other political prisoners. The door was very heavy and the iron bars of my windows were very thick, but nevertheless I managed to keep in touch with the outside world. I learnt that a team under the orders of two of our fighters, Mustapha Ikhlef and Boudissa, was planning my escape. But the team was up against a major difficulty: its plans were constantly being exposed and thwarted by the party leaders, who reckoned that I was quite all right where I was. In order to succeed, Ikhlef and Boudissa had therefore to elude the vigilance of the prison authorities and, at the same time, that of the leaders of my own party, which was far more difficult. But it would have needed more than this to discourage them; they were both remarkable fighters, loyal and courageous. Boudissa is still alive, and is today a member of the executive committee of the U.G.T.A.[1] But Ikhlef was captured the day after the events of the 1st November 1954, condemned to death and guillotined.

---

[1] Tr. note: *Union Générale de Travailleurs Algériens.*

4

The Revolution

At the end of March 1952, Boudissa came to see me at the prison grille and, through the intermediary of a warder, gave me a loaf of bread. Naturally, it was cut in half before being handed to me, according to the unchanging and useless routine of prisons. A strong file was hidden in one of the narrow ends of the long loaf.

We set to work at once, with the complicity of the sixty political prisoners in whose midst we were living. The fact that there was not one traitor among them to denounce us proves the value of our militant members of the *Organisation Spéciale*, and shows with what care they had been recruited.

If I remember rightly, it was my brother member, Kirkebane Ben Nasser who undertook, day after day, to file the bars of a window overlooking the prison yard. He was a mechanic by trade, and he accomplished his long task with remarkable skill. While his file was slowly wearing away the iron which separated us from freedom, the sixty prisoners sang in unison to drown the noise.

It had been agreed that only two of us, Mahsas and myself, would attempt to escape.[1] The prison yard was enclosed by a wall about sixteen feet high; but there was a second, much higher wall only a short distance away from the first. In the space between the two walls there

---

[1] Mahsas was made a minister by Ben Bella. He joined Colonel Boumedienne after the *coup d'état* of the 19th June 1965.

was a rampart-walk. It had been agreed that we would climb to the top of the first wall on a pyramid of prisoners, and that a rope would be thrown from outside to get us over the second one.

In all escapes there are surprises, usually nasty ones. We overcame the first obstacle without any difficulty. When I reached the top of the first wall, I saw to my inexpressible joy that the rope was already hanging over the second one at the agreed place. But at the same time I realized with horror that an electric fence about five feet wide ran along the far side of the wall on whose summit I was perched. It was therefore impossible to carry out our plan to hang by our hands and drop down the other side. It meant instead that we had to stand upright on top of the wall, and at the risk of either being electrocuted or breaking a leg, jump across a gap a good five feet wide, with a sixteen-foot drop on to the paving-stones of the rampart-walk below.

I went over first. I was in excellent physical shape, and made a perfect landing. But Mahsas was not so lucky. He twisted an ankle and hurt his arm on landing, and as I helped him up I realized that he would have the greatest difficulty in scaling the second wall. I went first and, taking hold of the rope and bracing both feet against the wall like a mountaineer, I reached the top. I shook the rope to signal to Mahsas that it was his turn. It was a fairly dark night and I could not see his face, but I guessed from his heavy breathing that he must be in terrible pain. I was sitting astride the top of the second wall, with one leg dangling alongside the rope so that he could grasp it when he reached my level. I would then be able to lean over, seize his hand, and pull him up.

At last I could see his face, a pale shape emerging from the darkness, and his hand, only about a foot below my ankle. But he failed to reach me, and fell back to the ground. I listened in the dark, and could hear him panting and groaning. I realized how much the effort had exhausted him. I leaned down and whispered to him to try again.

Twice again he climbed to within a yard of my ankle, and twice again he fell back to the ground. I was in despair, as I could do absolutely nothing to help him. I was leaning down towards him as far as I could without losing my balance, and all I could do was to wait until he could haul himself to the level of my leg. After his third attempt, he whispered to me from the foot of the wall: "You go ahead, Ahmed. You are safe." "No," I said, "try again."

I felt the rope tightening in my hand, and realized that he was making a fourth attempt. I could not believe that he would succeed as I had noticed how, after each try, he had dropped back further from his goal through exhaustion. But the will-power of a man who is really up against it can work miracles. I was staggered to see him suddenly rise up out of the darkness with a new burst of energy and grab hold of my ankle. I was overjoyed at his success, and seized his hand in both of mine: it was streaming with sweat. I pulled and heaved, and in a second he was sitting beside me on top of the wall, panting and bent double with exhaustion. After this it was child's play to throw the rope over the other side of the wall, and walk down into the sleeping town, down into freedom.

Our friends were waiting for us. They knew that it would not be long before our escape was discovered: a police net would be spread, and roads and railways would be watched. So they hit on the brilliant idea of hiding us in a place which nobody would dream of searching; in the house of one of our militant members, who lived within a short range of the prison, in a small house surrounded by a garden. As luck would have it, the wife of our fellow member was pregnant, and approaching the day of her confinement. The excitement of knowing that we were hidden in the house, when all the newspapers and the radio were full of the news of our escape, was too much for her, and she gave birth. This put us all in a most embarrassing situation: how was our host to celebrate with the traditional festivities which, in our country, always accompany the birth of a child—with two strangers hidden in the house? And how could he not hold the celebrations without immediately arousing the suspicions of the neighbours?

Having thought it over, our host decided to give the party. He hid us at the bottom of his garden in a shed made of reeds. In order to keep away the children, who would be sure to go ferreting in every corner after the feast, he gave us his fiercest dog for company. It was quite the ugliest, the most unfriendly, the most snarling and vicious member of the entire canine race. We spent a whole day threatening, beating, and cajoling it before it would even tolerate our presence, let alone accept us. It never stopped growling and casting hostile glances in our direction the whole time it was with us.

We were huddled together on an improvised bed, and we could hear everything that the women were saying in the nearby kitchen. The children came foraging close to our shed, but when this happened the dog would break out into such an outburst of barking, with blazing eyes and all his hackles up, and in such a state of rage, that we expected him to hurl himself upon us at any moment.

To complicate matters, Mahsas had caught cold during the escape and, without any warning, he would be seized with violent fits of coughing. I watched him going scarlet in the face, trying to stop the appalling tickle in his throat; he would just have time to say "Pillow!" to me, I would fling the pillow over his face, and he would burst out coughing again. Luckily the dog was so upset by this peculiar performance that he would burst out too, whereupon the women in the kitchen would start screaming to the children to come away from the dog.

When the party was over and the guests had gone home, the dog was taken away and all was quiet again. It was the end of March and spring had come to Blida, bringing flowers and filling the air with scent. Being free to breathe the evening air made us feel quite drunk, and seeing colours again enchanted us after the drab grey world of the prison, with its sunless yard and its great blank walls.

Our friends changed our hiding-place several times and then moved us to Algiers, where I became the hidden guest of a family of patriots. I wish that there were more families like this one in Algeria; from the youngest to the oldest they were all fighting for freedom, including the girls. When peace came, they carried on the fight, without thinking of their personal interests for a moment. I occasionally visit them and drink coffee with them round the family table, and we recall the six months which I spent with them after my escape. One of the girls, called Hassiba, is a wonderful, dedicated person; she looks after the shoe-shine boys and some of the sons of the *chouhadas*.[1]

In Algiers, my brothers of the *Organisation Spéciale* provided me with forged papers and, with the complicity of the crew, I sailed clandestinely in the steamship *Ville d'Oran*, bound for Marseilles. From there I went to Paris, where I hid for several months in a small room in the rue

---

[1] Algerians who were killed in the war. Their sons are brought up in state institutions. The shoe-shine boys were taken off the streets in February 1963.

Cadet, perched high up in Montmartre. I was certainly safer in Paris than I was in Algiers, but nevertheless I disciplined myself to going out very little, only when it was necessary to make vital contacts. I led a very quiet and recluse-like existence.

In 1953 I went to Egypt, where King Farouk had just been deposed, and where the first days of the Egyptian revolution were fraught with many difficulties. The beginning of our own revolution, in Cairo, was no easier. My friends and I were quite unknown in Egypt, and our life was very precarious. The bean is to the Egyptian what rice is to the Chinaman, and for four months beans were the only course of our one daily meal. A ready-cooked portion of beans cost, if I remember rightly, ten centimes; we could not afford anything else. At first we had some trouble in getting on with the Egyptian revolutionaries, because of language difficulties. I remember that the first time I spoke to the Arab League on the Algerian situation, I had to make my speech in French. French is unundoubtedly a magnificent language, but used in those surroundings it produced a disastrous effect. What scandal! What sacrilege! While I spoke to my Arab brothers, I could see their faces contorted with astonishment. I could well understand their feelings: the Arabic language is both the banner of our brotherhood, and our means of communication. But what could I do about it? I was an Algerian of the people, and the Algerian people had lived in darkness for so many centuries that they had forgotten how to speak the noble language of their ancestors.[1]

There were other differences of opinion between us and the Egyptians. Their plan was to create and finance a big North-African liberation movement, composed of three 'national sections'. This idea did not seem practical to

[1] The Algerian people speak an Arab dialect which is very different to classical Arabic.

me. The countries of the Maghreb[1] were far from being
united. How could we behave as though unity had
already been achieved, and at once begin to discuss the
delicate subject of a supra-national authority, at a time
when the fight for independence in all three countries of
the Maghreb was still undeniably a national one? We
refused to join in the project, and we explained our
reasons to our Egyptian friends. They took offence at
first, but later they were grateful to us for having stated
our point of view so clearly, and for our honesty in having
refused to accept subsidies from them, as we could not
agree to their plan. In the end, they reconsidered their
decision, and promised us all possible help with the
launching of our own insurrection.

We asked for nothing better! We were burning with
impatience. But Messali was sunk up to his beard in a
quagmire of ultra-conservatism. This had resulted in a
paradoxical situation, in which both Morocco and Tunisia
were already in a state of insurrection, but Algeria had
not moved. Both wings of the Maghreb were flapping,
but the body of the great bird remained still. The 'hard
core' of the party consisted of the ex-militant members of
the *Organisation Spéciale*, who had secretly reorganized
themselves and were in liaison with the *Extérieur* and
myself.[2] For months this hard core had been trying to
rouse the weak element to action, but all attempts had
failed. Turning their backs on history, Messali's supporters could only sit back and dream of elections.

The leaders of the *Organisation Spéciale* met during the
autumn of 1954 in Switzerland and decided, indepen-

---

[1] Tr. note: the Maghreb consists of the three countries of Morocco, Tunisia, and
Algeria.
[2] Tr. note: the *Extérieur* consisted of those members of the *Organisation Spéciale*
who had left Algeria and were operating from Europe or other Arab countries. The
Intérieur was composed of those who had remained to operate clandestinely in Algeria.

dently and without the knowledge of the party, to take action. We did not fix a definite date for the start of operations, as we did not wish to pin down our leaders of the *Intérieur*.[1] They themselves chose the 1st November, in deference to the local situation.

The Algerian Revolution started with a very small supply of arms; there were from 350 to 400 weapons in all,[2] most of them Italian muskets which had come from Libya. The *Organisation Spéciale* had experienced the greatest difficulty in smuggling them into Algeria, by a zigzag route from Tripoli to Ghadames and from Ghadames to Biskra. These guns had lain for more than a year buried in the Algerian soil which they were to help us to reconquer. They had been dug up at regular intervals, cleaned and greased, then once more carefully wrapped in cloths and buried again in a different place. None of our caches was ever discovered, and nobody betrayed us.

When the moment came, these arms were distributed more or less all over the country, but particularly in the Aurès mountains, where we planned to establish our principal revolutionary stronghold. No arms, however, were sent to the Oran district, because our Moroccan friends had promised to supply us there. A meeting-place was arranged somewhere in the Rif mountains, and at the agreed time and place our men arrived with their mules. They waited many long days, but nobody came. Our caravan returned empty-handed to the Oran area on the evening before the 1st November. Ramdane Abd-el-Malek, the leader of this district, was in despair. He had no means of informing the *Intérieur* leaders of this

[1] Footnote as on previouse page.
[2] In a telegram to Jacques Chevallier, General Cherrière spoke of "several thousand '*fusils de guerre*'." (Quoted by Claude Paillat in *Le Deuxième Dossier Secret de l'Algérie*, p. 56.)

dreadful blow to his hopes. Rather than appear as a
coward in their eyes, he attacked on the 1st November
with the negligible means at his disposal, and lost his life
in the attempt.

We anticipated two results from the action of the 1st
November. The first and most important was the long-
term result of rallying the entire Algerian people by
means of this action launched by a vigorous minority.
The second hoped-for result depended on the enemy
making a mistake: the mistake was duly made, as we had
anticipated, and we benefited enormously from it. We
knew that, if the situation became really serious, the
French government would not fail to dissolve the
M.T.L.D. and imprison its leaders. To our unspeakable
relief, this was exactly what happened. The government thereby relieved us of the presence of a lot of
political meddlers who were assumed to be our accomplices but who, in fact, were a terrible hindrance to our
movement because of the confusion which they created
in the mind of the public. On the 1st November, the
Organisation Spéciale had founded the *Front de Libération
Nationale* (the F.L.N.); now, thanks to the enemy, it
became the only political force in Algeria.

When Soustelle replaced Léonard, he realized the
extent of the blunder which his people had committed.
He at once set free some key figures, upheld the U.D.M.A.[1]
party of Ferhat Abbas, and made contact with its leaders.
Soustelle's plan was to secretly encourage a moderate
nationalist movement which would advocate some of the
same objectives as ourselves, but which were only to be
achieved through legal and constitutional means. It was
a clever idea, but it failed for two reasons. Firstly, because the protagonists of moderate nationalism, who

[1] Tr. note: *Union Démocratique du Manifeste Algérien.*

were all palpable opportunists, did not hesitate to contact us to cover themselves. On our part, we lost no time in telling them in plain terms that their political game would only be tolerated by us in so far as it could further our own activities. The second reason for the failure of Soustelle's plan became apparent less than a year after the 1st November, on the 20th August 1955. On this date, the anniversary of the deposing of Mohammed V, the insurrection of North Constantine took place, which proved to Algerian public opinion that the F.L.N., far from having been suffocated, had succeeded in spreading and intensifying its activities. The 'moderate nationalists' so dear to Soustelle thereupon reached the desired conclusions.[1]

While the insurrection developed, I was reorganizing logistical support for the operations, with the help of my friends of the *Extérieur*. The '*mousquetons*'[2] used on the 1st November could not for long support a guerrilla war. My task now was to obtain more serious armament in far greater quantities from other Arab countries, and to smuggle it into wartime Algeria.

Egypt had given us immense assistance from the start, and all the Arab countries helped us to a lesser degree. And I mean all the Arab countries, including even the least progressive ones such as Jordan and Saudi Arabia. The charming Queen Dina of Jordan even lent us her yacht to transport arms to the Moroccan coast, though at first this loan was, one might say, involuntary. When the crew was arrested by the Spanish after the operation, we had to confess to her the use to which her beautiful yacht had been put. She forgave us at once and, with

[1] Ben Bella is referring to the 'Manifesto of the Sixty-one'. Sixty-one elected Algerians met after the 20th August at the Palais Carnot, summoned by Ben Djelloul. They repudiated integration: thus, Soustelle's project lost all Algerian political foundation.
[2] Tr. note: the smaller French rifle used in artillery and cavalry units in 1939.

admirable good grace, she entered into the spirit of the game. She asked the Spaniards to release her yacht and its crew, assuring them that it was for her personal pleasure and under her orders that it was cruising without its owner, nearly two thousand miles away from its port of origin.

The yacht was called *Dina* after the Queen, and was a beautiful vessel. She was beached in a sandy creek off the Moroccan coast, in the middle of a February night of 1955. The sea was rough and the water was very cold. A rope was stretched from ship to shore and all night long our men, stripped naked and up to the armpits in icy water, carried heavy crates full of arms from the *Dina* to dry land. They were fighters from Marnia and Tlemcen who had crossed the frontier a fortnight previously and had lain low, dispersed among the villages of the Rif coast. Each man had to wade through two hundred yards of choppy sea, shivering with cold, and grasping the rope in one hand, while steadying the crate balanced on his shoulders with the other. There was no moon, and if he let go the rope, there was nothing to guide him but the short intermittent flash of an electric torch.

Some of the men were hurt and disabled, and some afterwards developed pneumonia; but by daybreak the *Dina* had been unloaded and the arms safely buried. During the following morning, the Rif peasants drove their flocks of sheep back and forth across the beach to remove all traces of the operation. Things began to go wrong when our men had to refloat the yacht. The Spanish police arrived, and their diver found two Mauser bayonets lying on the sea floor directly below the hull. The crew, as I have said, was arrested: but they shut up like clams. The inquiry was pursued in half-hearted fashion by the Spanish police. Queen Dina's energetic

The view across Algiers bay from Ben Bella's headquarters
(*London Express News and Feature Service*)

The Casbah, March 1962 (*Central Press*)

Improvised classroom for Arab children (*Central Press*)

intervention did not, possibly, entirely convince them; but she gave them the excuse which they wanted to be able to declare the matter closed.

After the *Dina* operation, there were two other very much more important ones: the second of these was carried out by an Egyptian battleship. This time it was not a question of '*mousquetons*', but of machine-guns, sub-machine-guns, mortars, bazookas, grenades, and large quantities of ammunition. The arms were of German and British origin and were, for the most part, new, modern, and up-to-date.

Thanks to this supply of arms, the Algerian insurrection was able to go into action on the 22nd October 1955 in the Oran district, the only region which, up to then, had been described in enemy reports as 'absolutely quiet'. A little later, the Ouarsenis mountain district rose in turn. The time had passed when the enemy could hope to crush the rebellion by isolating the Aurès mountain area. The F.L.N. was now fighting throughout the length and breadth of Algeria.

The Arab world too had begun to take up arms from one end of North Africa to the other. Our action in the Oran district had been carried out in liaison with Moroccan maquis fighters who were operating in the Rif and had even sent out columns in the direction of Taza and the Atlas mountains. In Algeria, the rising of North Constantine had sabotaged the Soustelle plan, and the impressive first moves made by Oran and the Rif on the 2nd October of that year had also upset the Grandval plan in Morocco. The enemy, for fear of losing everything, had to be content with cutting their losses. Mohammed V was hurriedly reinstated on his throne and Morocco was declared independent—within the limits, that is to say, of inter-dependence.

4

The independence of Morocco and also of Tunisia, which followed shortly afterwards, made a deep impression on the Algerians. Politically, it now seemed impossible to withhold from Algeria that which had already been granted to her neighbours. On the other hand, the cease-fire in Morocco raised a serious problem for us: the French army from now on would be free to concentrate on our activities. Our strategy was based on the wide dispersal of the French forces from one end of the Maghreb to the other. With the return of peace to Tunisia and Morocco, we would have to withstand the full force of their arms from now on, alone.

It cannot be denied that at this period some of the Algerian leaders showed a certain bitterness. We had pulled the chestnuts of independence out of the fire, but it was our brothers over the borders who were now enjoying eating them. But I knew that there was no sense in feeling bitter; we had to make the best of the situation and try to turn it to our advantage. I went to see Mohammed V in Madrid; he seemed unpretentious, intelligent, and completely honest. He was very worried about the effect which the cease-fire in Morocco would have on us. It is hardly exaggerating to say that he appeared to regret having agreed to it, for our sake; this was greatly to his credit, as he had no reason to reproach himself for anything. Our interview had important results; Mohammed V promised us all possible assistance, short of direct military aid. He gave us his solemn promise, amongst other things, that the Moroccan frontier would always be a friendly one to us, with access to it in both directions for our men and arms.

I continued, nevertheless, to direct boatloads of armaments to the Rif coast, with varying results. The most disastrous of these trips was that of the *Athos*, which was intercepted by the French navy. Understandably, the intense secret activity which these operations required involved me in all kinds of setbacks and dangers. Strangely enough, my first worries came, not from the French, but from the American secret service. The Americans must have considered us too 'radical' for their taste, as they set up their own intelligence network, which duplicated our own, and based it on the support of certain moderate elements among the *oulémas*[1] and in the U.D.M.A. This network was run by an American of Moslem origin operating from Libya.

It was obvious that the C.I.A.[2] had two objectives. One was to arm the Algerian nationalists against France (who, incidentally, was their ally in N.A.T.O.) in the hope of reaping rewards after Independence. The other was to strengthen the Algerian conservative faction, to the detriment of those Algerians who were suspected of socialism.

They achieved neither of these objectives. Although in fact the Americans did succeed in buying arms (in any case in insufficient quantity), and managed on one or two occasions to smuggle them successfully into Algeria, these arms were delivered to people who had not the slightest desire to fight, and who immediately buried them for ever. This network was hampering our own work in disastrous fashion. Its operators were noisy, talkative, corrupt, and overflowing with dollars. In addition, they led such dissipated lives that they were soon picked up by the French secret service, and by their ineptness they revealed to the French some of our own intelligence channels in Libya and Rome.

These amateurs were compromising us, so I decided to

[1] Tr. note: Moslem doctors of sacred law and theology.
[2] Tr. note: Central Intelligence Agency.

take action against them. In Rome, I met the American of Moslem origin who was behind them and, in the course of a violent scene, I threatened to liquidate his network unless he reduced his activities. To show him that I was not joking, I had his men in Morocco arrested and I did not release them until I had made him swear to fade into the background.

While I was harrying the Americans, I was myself being pursued by the French services. The first time they made themselves known to me was in Cairo, at the beginning of 1956. I was in my little office telephoning, when the *chaouch*[1] came in, carrying a parcel. I looked up: "What is that?" I said. "It's a parcel addressed in your name, which a taxi has just brought from the Semiramis Hotel." My 'name' was, of course, a pseudonym and it was known to very few people in Cairo. "Is the driver there?" I asked. "Yes, he is downstairs, waiting for his tip." "Give him his tip," I said, "and give him back the parcel. Tell him to take it back to whoever sent it. And hurry!"

But the bomb had been too exactly timed, and the taxi had hardly gone more than a few hundred yards when it exploded with a terrifying report. When the police arrived a few minutes later, they found the boot of the taxi hanging from a sixth-floor balcony. As for the unfortunate taxi-driver, who was the innocent victim of a war which he had never heard of—his body was blown to pieces.

When this happened, my friend Mahsas, who was responsible for security, said to me: "You really must look after yourself better. You are being very unwise, you are not even armed." Whereupon he stuffed a revolver

---

[1] Tr. note: in Egyptian Arabic, the word 'shaouish' means a policeman. Ben Bella is here probably referring to a door-keeper or watchman.

into my pocket. I shrugged my shoulders—the idea of a revolver against bombs! However, I kept it. I left Egypt for Libya, little knowing that a second trap awaited me in Tripoli.

Of all the Arab countries, I like Libya the best. Apart from my own countrymen, there are no people so attractive as the Libyans. They are simple, intelligent and affectionate; it is as though the beauty of the climate had entered into their souls. Whenever I think of them, I always wonder at their inexhaustible kindness, their capacity for friendship, and their purity of spirit. They have lived far from the turbulence of great cities and they have not been corrupted. In Libya, even the most reactionary bourgeois behaves in a way which is somehow attractive.

When I returned to Libya after Independence, the Libyans gave me an unforgettable welcome. Out of their kindness and generosity, and not knowing how else to express their friendship, they invested me with the honorary degree of Doctor of the University of Benghazi. I was half laughing and half moved, and as I embraced them I reminded them that my only qualification for this honour was my French diploma of the *certificat d'études*, a high-sounding name for such small achievement. But they refused to listen to me, and I became an honorary Doctor, through the kindness of the most affectionate people in the world.

In Tripoli in 1956, whenever I had some spare time between appointments, I used to walk in the big public garden of the town. It was here that, shortly before the 1st November 1954, I had arranged to meet Mustapha Ben Boulaïd, who later became the great leader of the insurrection in the Aurès mountains. As he had no papers, he had been forced to travel through the south of Tunisia, walking for days on end through the desert, half dead from thirst. When at last he arrived, exhausted and with bleeding feet, he was put in prison by the Libyan authorities. I found out where he was and soon managed to get him set free, and we spent ten days together making our plans. We were both so poor that the public garden of Tripoli was our only dining-room, and bread and grapes our only food. But faith in a better world kept us alive.

Ben Boulaïd came to see me again at the beginning of 1955, but this time he was arrested by Tunisian policemen. While struggling to free himself, he killed one of the policemen. He got away, but he was finally caught, handed over to the French authorities, and condemned to death. By some miracle he succeeded in escaping on the 4th November of the same year, and rejoined his *maquisards* in the Aurès mountains. He had only been there a few months and was busy reorganizing his men, when one day some *fellaheen* brought him a radio transmitting set, which they had found at some distance from an outpost. It had been parachuted 'by mistake' from a French plane. Ben Boulaïd unpacked it himself, set it up in front of him, and turned the starting-knob. It was full of plastic high explosive, and Ben Boulaïd was blown to pieces.

I was walking sadly by myself in the garden where, two years before, we had eaten our frugal meals together. I remembered Ben Boulaïd's serenity, his spiritual strength, and his patience in the face of ordeals. With my mind full of memories of this great fighter, little did I guess that, even now, death was lying in wait for me too in Tripoli.

Death with a name, and a face, called Jean David. This man was a French *colon* living in Tunisia. He had joined the *Main Rouge*, and why he had been appointed my executioner, only those who employed him at that time could tell us today. Whether or not it was entirely a by-product of the French secret service, the *Main Rouge* was causing a great deal of talk at that time, and it had pulled off several *coups* against our people, in Germany in particular.

In any case, Jean David was an efficient killer. As the inquiry was to show, he prepared his plot against me with great care as, knowing that I was in touch with the Libyan government, he assumed that I had far greater protection than I in fact had. It was true that I was in liaison with the Libyans and that they were giving me real help, but this had been kept absolutely secret, as Libya was still under foreign influence and the chief of police was an Englishman. I had therefore to work in complete secrecy, unknown to either the police or the Libyan security services.

Jean David took six months to prepare his *coup*. He passed himself off as the representative of a commercial firm, driving regularly backwards and forwards between Tunis and Tripoli. The Libyan customs and police control grew used to seeing him in his car at all hours of the day and night, always polite and affable. The Libyans were grateful to this European for his good manners and became, so to speak, acclimatized to his frequent journeys across the frontier. Gradually they allowed him to dispense with the tedious formalities which a foreigner must undergo when crossing a frontier by car. This conditioning of the Libyan officials was very important to Jean David as, once he had struck, his safety would depend on getting back into Tunisia as quickly as possible.

There are certain capital cities which seem cut out to be battle-grounds for secret agents, but Tripoli is not one of these. The town is so quiet and pleasant and the people so peace-loving that, at a pinch, it could manage without a police force. I was living in an hotel called the Excelsior, which was clean, but quite small. The manager always went to bed early, and the only protection at night was from a night-watchman, who did very little watching. I was usually very late coming home at night, as all my appointments had to be after dark. I never failed to find the night-watchman asleep behind his desk.

When I got back to the Hotel Excelsior that night at about one o'clock, I noticed a car parked outside the entrance. I recognized it as belonging to a European whom I had passed on leaving the hotel earlier in the evening. I noticed briefly that the back seat was piled with luggage, as though the owner of the car was preparing to leave.

The night-watchman was of course fast asleep, so I took my key without waking him, and walked upstairs to the first floor. I opened my bedroom door, put my hand through the doorway, and turned on the light switch. Nothing happened. I thought to myself, "The bulb must have gone", and took a step forward into the room. At the same instant I sensed that hardly perceptible feeling of warning which tells one, usually a quarter of a second too late, that danger is threatening. I stopped, absolutely still. Perhaps my assailant was conscious of my moment of hesitation; in any case he did not wait for me to shut the door. He struck—and he struck too soon, not on the back of my neck as he should have done, but on the side of my head. It was a terrible blow, but it did not fell me and I did not lose consciousness. I lashed out with my fist in his direction and hit him. He hit me too, and I felt that I was going to faint. Then I remembered Mahsas' revolver: I jumped back, dropped to the floor, and fired.

Ben Bella, with Colonel Boumedienne on his right, September 1962; Boumedienne's entry into Algiers at the head of Willayas I and VI was marked by celebrations (*Keystone Press*)

Ben Bella takes his place in the General Assembly of the United Nations, October 1962 (*Central Press*)

I fired a full round, haphazard, in his direction without hitting him. I think he must have fired back at me, as the window behind me was shattered; the shots rang out with a deafening noise. I could see the man's body darkly outlined against the lighter rectangle of the door, and I knew that he had escaped.

I staggered to my feet, felt something warm running down the side of my face and, forgetting that my revolver was now empty, I ran after him. I reached the top of the stairs, tripped over the first step, and fell from the top to the bottom in a dead faint.

The alarm had been given by telephone, and a barrier was put up on the main road. Jean David charged the barrier, the police gave way, and let him pass. But he made one mistake: he relied too much on the good nature of the Libyan officials. He came to the second barrier a few miles from the frontier and tried to crash it in the same way as the first one. Shots were fired, and he was killed.

My wound was cleaned and dressed, and I quickly recovered. Fate had given me a reprieve. There were other alarms in Rome, but nothing serious. I relied on my mobility for protection; I never spent long in the same town, as I was usually travelling round, organizing our arms supplies. I literally lived in aeroplanes, as I was always flying backwards and forwards between Cairo, Tripoli, Rome, Madrid and Tetuan.

I remember that, when I took my seat in an aeroplane and fastened my safety-belt, I always felt that here at any rate there was some respite for me. I could feel completely safe for a few hours.

I was wrong about this, as I was to learn in a very short time.

5

Capture

Before describing my arrest, I would like to go back a little and recall the serious political results of the Congress of Soummam.[1]

The Congress undeniably gave to the Revolution the structure, the hierarchy, and the organization which it lacked. But at the same time it also introduced bureaucracy and red tape, which succeeded in gradually detaching the movement from the realities of the struggle. The main error of the Congress was in appointing to executive posts politicians who had always opposed the transition to armed rebellion, and who had not hesitated to publicly denounce our action after the 1st November. Nevertheless, when they saw the success of our armed forces and the impressive progress of the F.L.N., these unmitigated opportunists 'evolved'. They now started to jump on the band wagon and profit from the Revolution which they had at first treated with so much scorn.

The leadership of the F.L.N. now became full of confusion and contradiction, and was noticeably lacking in strong principles and well thought-out revolutionary strategy. Our capture a few months later left the field clear for the politicians, both left-wing and conservative,

[1] The Congress of Soummam took place in Kabylia on 20th August 1956. It was very cleverly organized by the Kabyle chief, Krim Belkacem. The Congress modified the executive organization of the Algerian Revolution, giving precedence to the *Intérieur* at the expense of the *Extérieur*. It reduced the powers of Ben Bella and the 'historical leaders' of the 1st November, and gave the lead to moderate nationalists who, like Ferhat Abbas, had somewhat tardily joined the F.L.N.

who had none of the training required for the organizing of a revolution.

They therefore made some mistakes during the revolutionary war which were almost catastrophic. They were unable to assess correctly the value of the respective parts played by the towns and the country districts in guerrilla warfare. They could not understand that the town-dwellers, living at close quarters and so to speak integrated with the enemy, whose vast repressive system surrounded them on all sides, could not possibly stage a mass rebellion without being instantly crushed, their network dismantled, their apparatus destroyed, and their fighters arrested or killed. Because they understood none of this, the leaders were foolish enough to take on the army of occupation in the battle of Algiers. As we know, it resulted in a heavy defeat for our people, which demolished our town network and consequently isolated and weakened the guerrilla forces of the country districts.

Another mistake was made, this time through the left-wing members overplaying their hands: this was the school strike. F.L.N. orders were, that on a certain day all the children were to walk out of our French secondary schools, and all undergraduates were to boycott lectures and examinations in the French universities. This was an inept measure, which did not worry or hurt the adversary but, on the contrary, did us enormous harm. At a moment when we were going to be in the greatest need of an educated class, our students and undergraduates, and consequently the future Algerian state, were to lose months and years of work.

But my main grievance against the executive personnel elected by the Congress of Soummam is for having left the *willayas* without arms, medicine, or money. I know of course that the frontier network of electrified fences made smuggling more difficult by the land route. But there was still the sea route, with hundreds of miles of coastline; this could have been far more extensively used for smuggling by the people in charge of the logistical organization of the Revolution.

The *willayas* deteriorated in predictable fashion, because they were abandoned, and left without arms and without orders. They had to fall back on their own resources, as they had no contact with the *Extérieur*; they were sometimes even cut off from each other, and they were living in a state of autarchy in districts which they had come to consider as being held by them in fief. In these districts, some of the commandants had acquired the mentality of feudal chieftains and gang leaders. Whilst condemning the system of *'willayisme'* and its terrible results at the time of Independence, it can never be sufficiently stressed that the primary responsibility for these mistakes did not lie with the *willayas* themselves. They must at least be given credit for having kept up the struggle under the most difficult conditions. The fault lies with the bureaucratic system which was more concerned with its international relations and with personal rivalries, and did not give enough attention to those who were fighting in the field.

Now I come to the circumstance of my capture. On the 22nd October 1956, the Moroccan plane which was to take the principal leaders of the *Extérieur* and myself from Rabat to Tunis was deflected from its itinerary, with the complicity of the French crew. The order was given over the radio by the French General Staff in Algeria. The plane landed at Algiers, where an armoured squadron and hordes of police awaited us.

Those are the facts. In order to understand them it is

necessary to look at them in the political context of that
time.

We had been in contact for a year with the government
of Guy Mollet, in the hope of putting an end to the
Algerian war by means of a negotiated peace. There had
been five meetings, one in Cairo, two in Belgrade and
two in Rome.

The last meeting in Rome had occupied part of the
month of September 1956. Our contact, Monsieur Com-
min, was not, if I remember correctly, a member of the
French government. But he was assistant secretary-
general of the S.F.I.O., and was therefore in very close
touch with Premier Guy Mollet, and he had been invested
by him with all the necessary powers.

In September, agreement was finally reached. It was
decided that both parties would return home to have the
agreement ratified. This done, we would meet again in
Rome to complete the negotiations and make them valid
and public.

To return home, for us, meant obtaining safe-conducts
from the French for two of our people to enter Algeria, in
order to inform our fighters of the *Intérieur* of the conditions which we had been offered. Much to our surprise,
Guy Mollet's government was not at all forthcoming on
this matter. Clearly, they were not very certain at that
moment of being able to count on the obedience of the
army. Nevertheless, when we insisted, they promised us
our *laissez-passer*.

We believed that peace was in reach when, without the
knowledge of Guy Mollet, Lacoste and the army perpetrated this act of international piracy, which became
known as the 'aeroplane *coup*'. The French government,
faced with the *fait accompli*, weakly accepted it. By doing
so, it gave in to the army and, with its own hands, buried

all hope of the peace which it had wanted and, by the same act, condemned in the long run those very institutions from which that same government had sprung. What bloodshed and what suffering could have been avoided if the French government had stood firm! The Algerians would have been spared six years of war and the appalling losses which resulted. And France would not have suffered the terrible convulsions which brought her to the verge of ruin, and from which she has even now hardly recovered.

It is worth recalling the chain of apparently trifling events which led to our presence in that Moroccan plane on the 22nd October 1956. Following our negotiations with the French government emissary in Rome, it had been agreed that we would hold a further meeting in Tunis, at which the three North African states would be represented. Tunisia and Morocco had both supported the effort of the Algerian Revolution; out of courtesy, and for the sake of our friendship with them, we wished to inform them of the peace terms which we had been offered.

Before doing this, we held a meeting of our leaders in Madrid; during our stay in the Spanish capital, an emissary of Prince Moulay Hassan came to tell us that the Sultan would like to see us at Rabat. To myself at least, the prospect of this journey did not appeal. Morocco was still occupied by French troops; the *Main Rouge*, which was later to reveal its presence in the country by means of horrifying murders, was already showing signs of considerable activity. However, we felt too much respect for the Sultan to be able to refuse his invitation.

At Rabat, it was agreed that we should go to Tunis with Mohammed V, to hold our Maghrabian conference. Although the plane was a Moroccan one the crew, as I

have said, was French; but the presence of the Moroccan
sovereign in the same plane seemed sufficient guarantee
of our safety. Unfortunately, at the last moment the
Palace informed us that there would not be room for us
in His Majesty's plane, and that a second one would be
placed at our disposal. I did not like the sound of this.
But it was already the 22nd of October and the Tunis
meeting had been fixed for the 23rd. There was not
enough time left to fly to Tunis via Madrid; so we accepted the Palace offer. The outlook at that moment was
hopeful, and peace seemed imminent: we felt that the
French government, apparently so eager to sign, could
surely not wish to sabotage the peace by allowing a plot
against us. Here, in short, lay our mistake. We had over-
estimated the enemy government, its coherence, the
loyalty of its ministers and its army towards their chief,
and the ability of that chief to command their obedience.

We believed, therefore, that we had no reason to fear
anything. But instinct, which, under the circumstances,
would have been a better guide than reason, would not
let me relax. As we took off from Rabat airport in the
D.C.3 which was to take us to Tunis, I confided to Khider
that I felt apprehensive. "Oh you!" he answered teas-
ingly, "you're always suspicious!" I believe that he was
wrong there, because it is not in my nature to be always
on my guard. I am in fact far from being as careful as I
should be, considering the heavy responsibilities which I
bear, and knowing that I am exposed to so much enmity.

On that day, however, I did feel some suspicion; but
I felt it too late. My misgivings in the plane increased
when I noticed the behaviour of the air-hostess. On
arrival, I had put my revolver into the pocket which was
on the back of the seat facing me: I am not sure whether
she saw me doing this, but she hovered round me for

quite a little while. Finally, she even touched the zip-fastener of the pocket. I stopped her. "Leave that alone!" I said sharply, "I have put my things in there." She started back, looking rather embarrassed, and without a word went to the pilot's cabin. I realized that she had gone to report.

I learnt afterwards that the enemy had contacted the French pilot over the radio, and had asked him to land at Oran. The pilot had at first refused, and had even informed the Moroccan authorities of the pressure which was being put on him. Rabat ordered him to return at once to Morocco. What happened then? Did this order never reach the pilot? Or had he already decided to give us up to the French?

Whatever the truth of it was, when the D.C.3 called at the Majorcan airport of Palma, Rabat already knew that there had been an attempt to alter the course of the plane. In the absence of their sovereign, who was ahead of us in the other plane, had the Palace officials lacked the initiative to take action? This is quite possible, as one would think that they could have asked the Spanish authorities to detain the aeroplane, which was a Moroccan one, at Palma airport.

I learnt afterwards that what made the French pilot hesitate for a long time was the fear of reprisals against his family living in Morocco. It appears that he only gave in to the very strong pressure which was put on him over the radio when the French General Staff gave him their word that his family would at once be given protection by the French services in Morocco. It was then, and only then, that he decided to submit.

Our actions often have far removed and unpredictable consequences. The pilot, reassured as to the fate of his own family, could not know that his decision was to cost

the lives of other French families, who became the innocent victims of the unreasoning rage of the Moroccan
masses, when they learnt of the insult to their sovereign.[1]

Shortly after the Palma stop, it seemed to me that the
plane was not on its usual course and was heading in a
too southerly direction. I remarked on this to the air-
hostess. Again she looked embarrassed, and replied: "It
is possible that we are taking a more direct route." I
jumped up. "What do you mean by more direct? We are
surely not going to fly over Algeria, are we?" "No, no,"
she said hurriedly, "but we may be taking a short
cut."

I will not attempt to describe my feelings when, as we
came in to land, I saw that the 'short cut' was Algiers
airport. I jumped up, boiling with rage, and seized my
revolver from the pocket. "No, no," said one of our
friends, with his hand on my arm, "leave your gun where
it is. You must not give them such a beautiful excuse."

Then came our arrest at Algiers airport. What a turn-
out, just to capture five men! There were two French-
women in the plane, Eve Deschamps of *France-Observa-
teur*, and Christiane Darbor. They were indignant at the
piracy which they had witnessed, and they went for the
police with such vehemence that they too were arrested.
They were fairly roughly handled, and bundled into the
same prison van as ourselves. But this did not discourage
them, and they continued to protest.

The atmosphere inside the prison van was ominous.
We were preceded and followed by the growling noise of
tanks and the roar of motor-bicycles, and the van was full
of policemen. They threatened and insulted us, and we
were packed so tight in among them that we could hardly
move. We were convinced that we were going to be

[1] A reference to the Meknès rising.

murdered, with the tacit approval of the authorities. We stopped talking, as we did not want to waste our last moments in pointless conversation.

Our silence finally impressed the guards and they also stopped talking. At that moment, Eve Deschamps drew closer to me and, without a word, seized my hand and held it. It was such a brave and generous gesture, that I can find no expression of thanks in any language which is worthy of it.

We were taken to the police station of El Biar,[1] where we were interrogated in succession by all the police forces which existed in Algiers at that time—and heaven knows there were plenty of them! After that it was the army's turn. A general came to see us: I do not know his name, as he did not introduce himself to his prisoners. He particularly wanted to know our views on the future of the war, now that we were prisoners. He was rather surprised to find that we were very optimistic.

A colonel came to see us a few days later. Oh those colonels! What harm they did to Algeria!

This one, however, seemed to be quite a worthy fellow. It was the 29th October: France and England had attacked Egypt. He explained to us that they were going to fix Nasser; we were already fixed. So, there would be no more revolution in Egypt, no more revolution in Algeria. Everything would be in order again. I looked at him in amazement. Soldiers are sometimes very simple.

When my turn came to speak, I told him that there are many other 'forces' in the world besides 'force': that there is the power of public opinion and international agreements, and the hopes and yearnings of the masses. I told him that the Algerian Revolution had advanced

[1] A residential quarter on the heights of Algiers.

beyond the stage when its fate depended on four or five leaders, and that, far from everything being over, things had only just begun. But he shook his head, and always came back to the same point: no more Nasser, no more Ben Bella; the whole question was settled.

The attitude of certain of the police towards us during the eight to ten days which we spent in Algiers was very disagreeable: they poured scorn upon us. I remember that when we were made to give an interview to the press, one of them referred to me derisively as *"Monsieur le Président du Conseil"*. I took advantage of the presence of the journalists to protest against the humiliations which were heaped on us every day. I added, that they could do anything they liked to us, including shooting us "while attempting to escape", but that nothing, neither threats nor outrages, could shake our resolution. I told them that we were not afraid of death or captivity, and that whatever happened, the Algerian Revolution would carry on without us and would triumph in the end.

There were about forty journalists listening to me that day: not one of them reported my speech. I had plenty of opportunity to observe the well-known 'objectivity' of the western press in action. Some of them even went so far as to parody my words and reduce the whole interview to the level of a petty incident by writing: "Ben Bella complained because a policeman called him *'Monsieur le Président'*."

About ten days later, the order came to transfer us to the Santé prison in Paris. We made the journey by air, in handcuffs, and with a policeman on either side of each of us. They had evidently been given very strict orders, as none of them opened their mouths; they did not even answer when one of us complained several times that the handcuffs were too tight.

At the Santé we were at first put under strict surveillance; every two minutes throughout the twenty-four hours a little shutter opened, and the eye of a guard observed us. We learnt that the prison authorities were afraid of suicide. What an incredible lack of insight this showed! A true revolutionary does not commit suicide. He is the interpreter of the deepest hopes of a whole nation, and he cannot despair of victory.

I spent six years in prison, and six years is a very long time. But I do not regret it; it strengthened and matured me enormously. For a fighter who has been unlucky, there is no more honourable place than prison. Even now, I would be prepared to go back there, rather than betray the cause which I serve.

The worst part of our captivity was certainly the two and a half years which we spent in the Santé. Then, in March 1959, de Gaulle had us transferred to the Island of Aix,[1] where our living conditions improved.

We were moved again, from the Island of Aix to Turquant on the Loire, where we remained from March 1961 until the end of December of the same year. Our last home was at Aulnoy where, through our friends of the *Extérieur*, we were able to follow the vicissitudes of the Evian negotiations.

We went on several hunger-strikes in our various prisons; the sole object of all these strikes was to safeguard, for ourselves and our brothers, the status of political prisoners.

We survived all our hunger-strikes by drinking water,

---

[1] When de Gaulle announced this transfer to his cabinet, Guillaumat said: "It seems to me, General, that it is only my duty to warn you that no doubt the Army, and the French in Algeria will not understand. . . ." "There have always been measures of clemency," snapped de Gaulle. "As for the Army, it is made to obey orders. And as for the French in Algeria, well, they are Frenchmen like all the rest, and like all the rest, they have got to obey the government." (Claude Paillat in *Dossier Secret de l'Algérie*, Vol. I, p. 174.)

because without water one cannot go on for very long, and we had to last out for as long as possible in order to rouse public opinion and worry the authorities sufficiently to influence their decisions. The hunger-striker is a special kind of fighter; his object is, not to kill the enemy, but to shame him by killing himself. By his slow suicide, he harrows the enemy with feelings of responsibility for his eventual death. At Turquant, our final hunger-strike lasted for twenty-two days and landed us in hospital at Garches. It was a sympathetic strike, as Debré had tried to go back on the rights of some of our political prisoners in certain prisons. It was a unanimous movement: fifteen thousand Algerians, women included, went on strike at the same moment. There were no defections. This showed great courage, when one realises the terrible danger, and the agony, caused by starvation.

One interesting aspect of our imprisonment was that, through the force of circumstances, our jailers also became our protectors because of the constant threats to our lives. French extremists considered it scandalous that we were still alive, and were plotting to kidnap and execute us. On the 13th May 1958, a 'Committee of Public Safety', taking advantage of the unrest of that moment, came to the Santé to 'take us in charge'. They met with a most emphatic refusal, and beat a retreat rather than risk their necks to get us.

Rumours of plots persisted, and at one moment in the Island of Aix we had two hundred mobile police to guard us. They took the most extraordinary precautions, and when we expressed surprise they did not hide from us that these precautions were not to prevent us from escaping, but rather to preserve our lives.

At Turquant, and then at Aulnoy, as peace drew slowly nearer the most incredible rumours circulated. It was said that the O.A.S.[1] was preparing a spectacular attack on us. There was even talk, at one moment, of rockets fired from aeroplanes. I do not know if the French government had provided an anti-aircraft battery to defend us, but certainly the vigilance of the mobile police who surrounded us was very impressive. On our side, we had also taken steps. Thanks to our contact with the outside world, commandos had been organized which were ready to act at a moment's notice.

In the end, nothing happened. The only victim, as everyone knows, was a man who had nothing whatever to do with the Algerian Revolution, the unfortunate Mayor of Evian. It was a completely pointless murder, which did not even hold up the negotiations for an hour.

During all the time of our captivity, the news which continued to reach us from the *Extérieur* worried me profoundly. It had certainly been necessary to create the G.P.R.A.[2] but its duration and its influence should have been limited, and it should not have been built up into an apparatus which was daily degenerating into a political mandarinate. The G.P.R.A., in fact, was behaving like a government and its leaders were already acting the parts of ministers. They devoted more attention to diplomatic battles than to the often despairing cries for help which came from the fighters of the *Intérieur*.

From this time onwards, two situations existed side by side in the Algerian Revolution. One, which was atrocious, was that of the fighters of the *Intérieur* and the frontier refugees. The other was the glittering and sumptuous way of life of certain ministers of the G.P.R.A.,

---

[1] *Organisation de l'Armée Secrète*. Formed by extreme right-wing elements which tried to replace the legal authorities of France after the upheaval in the French army in Algiers.
[2] In order to facilitate their international relations, the leaders of the *Extérieur* formed themselves into the *Gouvernement Provisoire de la République Algérienne*.

who were already living in the same fashion as some African régimes which I prefer not to mention by name. To sum up, it was clear that the Revolution would be replaced, immediately after Independence, by a facile and corrupt régime which, installed with official blessings and amid widespread intrigue, would leave the people to struggle in their misery.

It is no secret that I was at first very much against the Evian agreements, as I considered them to be too Draconian. In spite of this, I agreed to sign them after modifications had been made at our suggestion. I gave my consent on one condition: that the G.P.R.A. should undertake to summon a congress immediately after the cease-fire, for the purpose of establishing the policy of the future government.

Incredible though it may seem, our liberation was the subject of a serious difference of opinion between the French government and ourselves. De Gaulle, wishing to make an elegant and courteous gesture to Morocco, wanted to hand us over to Hassan II. I absolutely refused to agree to this: I had already burned my fingers twice, and I did not want to fly over North Africa once again in a French plane. The Elysée insisted. I also insisted, and I said to their envoy: "Am I a parcel? Am I just an object, which is to be put down in the exact place where it was picked up? Oh no: I want to choose where I am going, and I want to go to Switzerland, not Morocco."

The argument lasted a good five days. At one moment they even threatened to move us under military orders and take us by force to Rabat. Finally, the Elysée gave way. Our departure from Aulnoy on the 19th March 1962 was organized by a master hand. A first convoy set off without us, in order to hoodwink the press and the O.A.S. A second convoy took us by a roundabout route to Orly.

I had been living cut off from the world for six years, with no window onto the outside. But during my absence the world had been transformed, and France had made technical progress. I was dazzled by the Caravelle in which we took our seats. The elegant lines of the machine appealed to me at once. When we took off, I experienced a marvellous sensation of power and of taking flight, which somehow confused itself in my mind with the intoxicating knowledge that I was once more free.

Ben Bella with President Kennedy, during a reception at the White House in his honour (*Keystone Press*)

Triumphant tour with Fidel Castro in Cuba (*Keystone Press*)

Ben Bella recognizes an old friend and introduces him to one of his officers—a scene typical of Ben Bella's tours in the villages of Algeria (*London Express News and Feature Service*)

6

The Aftermath of Independence

As soon as we landed in Geneva, the Swiss took charge of us and drove us to the offices of the *Signal de Bougie*, where the G.P.R.A. awaited us. The *Signal de Bougie* building was on the opposite side of the lake facing Evian, where the negotiations had taken place. It was a real fortress, surrounded by barbed wire and guarded by the Swiss police, with helicopters constantly flying overhead.

After six years imprisonment, this was our first contact with reality, and we found it a bitter experience. The gentlemen of the G.P.R.A. were not at all delighted to see us again; on the surface their welcome was friendly enough, but its depths were icy cold. I only spent two or three days at the *Signal de Bougie*, as the atmosphere of intrigue was suffocating. There were nothing but sidelong glances, forced laughter, and whispering behind one's back.

The Moroccans, on the other hand, were most anxious to welcome us; they had purposely hired a Boeing to take us from Geneva to Rabat. But there was a last-minute hitch; the French government, who had not forgiven us for having prevented their gesture of courtesy to the Sultan, now forbade our unfortunate Boeing to fly over

French territory. So we had to go all the way round by
Italy, and cross the Mediterranean from east to
west.

In Morocco, our welcome from the crowds was excellent; we went from there to Egypt, where it was marvellous, and from Egypt to Irak, where it was delirious. But
I realised that this delirium, so friendly towards ourselves, included some brick-bats for Kassem: boos for
him were mixed with cheers for us. Our route from the
airport to the Palace was blocked by an impenetrable,
surging crowd. The demonstrators jumped on the bonnet
and the boot, and pressed against the windows of the
car. Glowering, they shouted anti-Kassem slogans, which
from time to time they would interrupt with beaming
smiles and praise for our victory. I have never seen a
crowd which was so easily able to jump with spon-
taneous agility from execration to enthusiasm.

After this demonstration, Kassem put us in a palace
where he kept us isolated from the outside world. He
lived himself in the furthermost recesses of a barracks
from which he never emerged, surrounded by troops of
whose loyalty he could never be certain. His régime was
like a wooden house whose walls were being eaten away
from the inside by termites: he too was eaten up by
worry. It was almost impossible to have a consecutive
conversation with him; he was consumed by an incredible
feverish restlessness. He would change the subject every
ten minutes, get up and walk aimlessly round and round
the room and then sit down, only to jump up again. It
was quite clear that his nerves (and perhaps his mind too)
were in a thoroughly unhealthy state, and that he had
lost all self-control. The little that I was able to grasp of
his political beliefs horrified me.

It will be remembered that when I was at Aulnoy, I

had insisted that the G.P.R.A. should summon a congress immediately after our liberation. The sovereignty
of Algeria had been recognised, but only as a formality,
and the reality could take many shapes. Here lay the
weakness of the F.L.N.: it had neither policy nor doctrine.
The Algerian Revolution had been one without ideology,
a lack which in wartime had allowed of widespread unity
in the fight against colonial power. But this absence of
ideology caused a void which, once peace returned,
became dangerous because the Evian agreements (if carried a stage further) already implied a marriage of neo-
colonialist character. It was necessary to extricate ourselves from this underhand marriage contract (which
would all the same have been very reassuring to certain
members of the G.P.R.A.), and to give purpose and
direction to our Independence.

At Aulnoy, we had drawn up a programme which
implicitly envisaged a socialist structure in Algeria. The
representatives of both the *Intérieur* and the *Extérieur*
were now able to meet for discussions for the first time.
It was the presence of these fighters which enabled us to
decide on a future programme. In fact, there was very
little opposition of any importance, not because all the
congressmen were socialists, but because those who were
not doubtless felt that there was a big difference between
a programme and its actual realization.

Things began to go wrong when it became clear that
the Congress was about to elect a *Bureau Politique* which
would not include any members of the G.P.R.A. The
G.P.R.A. then seized on a dispute between the congressmen as an excuse for them to resign from the Congress,
and they then declared that they considered it to be null
and void.

The cynicism and the impudence of their behaviour

flabbergasted us. Their attitude was "Very well: we re-sign. And as we have resigned, nothing has happened, nothing has been decided, no programme has been voted for, and there has been no Congress."

My colleagues were so outraged by this manœuvre, that they wanted straight away to announce officially the composition of the *Bureau Politique*. At first, I was the only one who objected to this proceedure, but in the end my opinion prevailed. The O.A.S. was still very strong, particularly in the Oran district, where certain of its members wanted to form a separate area, thereby creating a kind of stronghold where they could remain indefinitely. Then again, in Algiers the *Exécutif Provi-soire*,[1] which had largely emanated from the French government, had at its disposal a local force consisting of former *harkis*[2] and sharp-shooters. In principle, this force was intended for use against the O.A.S.; but it could have played a very different part had there been an open split in the F.L.N., with rival factions in a perpetual state of disagreement.

It would have been a mistake to announce the compo-sition of the *Bureau Politique* in opposition to the G.P.R.A. at the close of the Congress of Tripoli, before the proclamation of Independence by referendum. It would have been playing into the hands of the O.A.S. and encouraging it in its dreams of partition, and it would also have encouraged the *Exécutif Provisoire* to remain in power for ever by continuing to act the part of arbitrator.

---

[1] According to the Evian agreements, the *Exécutif Provisoire*, presided over by Monsieur Farès, was to administer current affairs until Algeria had elected her repre-sentatives and formed her government. Monsieur Farès was a very moderate nationalist, with whom the French government had kept in contact throughout the Algerian war.

[2] Tr. note: the *harkis* were Algerians who had been recruited by the French army during the war of Algeria to fight against their own countrymen, and who were con-sidered by them to be traitors.

It was therefore decided that the irremediable breach which had occurred in the heart of the F.L.N., for which the G.P.R.A. was directly responsible, would not be made public until after the results of the referendum were known. The referendum, in fact, by proclaiming the Independence of Algeria, with the practically unanimous support of the masses, would bring about a situation in which both from the internal and the international points of view, neither the O.A.S. nor the *Exécutif Provisoire* could raise the issue afresh.

My colleagues and I therefore joined the members of the G.P.R.A. in Tunis where, as may be imagined, our welcome was not exactly warm. The G.P.R.A. knew that the game was still open, and they were more determined than ever to hang on to power. The Provisional Government of the Republic of Algeria had already been recognized by a number of countries, and took courage from its organization, from its good relations with the press, and from its secret alliances. It meant to use the Revolution for its own ends, and to shelve the Tripoli Programme.

The G.P.R.A. were particularly on their guard against the A.L.N.,[1] because they suspected its General Staff of progressive tendencies. Even before the referendum, they had started 'parachuting' emissaries to the *willayas*, who had orders either to take charge, or to stiffen the *willayas* against the A.L.N., by persuading them that the A.L.N., in returning to Algeria, was planning a putsch to liquidate them and install a military régime. This was how the famous 'autonomous zone' of Algiers was created, to operate both against the A.L.N. and myself. In a few days, the walls of the Casbah were plastered with slogans

---

[1] In Morocco, and more particularly in Tunisia, the *Armée de Libération Nationale* had remained in those countries, having been unable to penetrate the electrified frontier defences. The A.L.N. represented a well-equipped and well-disciplined force of considerable strength. But it was somewhat looked down on by the fighters of the *willayas* for not having taken part in the fighting in Algeria.

warning the people against building up a personality cult around me, and announcing that there was "only one hero —the people"! I was then, and am now incidentally, in full agreement with this political formula, with one reservation: the G.P.R.A. was not worrying overmuch about the people when it had the effrontery to incite the Algerians against me.

The internal activities of the G.P.R.A. were characterized by the worst reaction. Algerian soil had hardly been liberated before they were busy arresting the bravest and most noteworthy of our fighters, amongst whom were Boualem and Djemila Bouhired, one of the heroes of the battle of Algiers.

In Tunis, while the outlook of the G.P.R.A. gradually hardened, I could feel their hostility towards me growing stronger, and my movements were watched. In fact, I fully expected an attack, so I decided to put myself out of their reach. One day, without any warning, and without telling a soul, I took off in a special Egyptian plane which was leaving Tunis. The departure was delayed by half an hour, and I learnt afterwards that the G.P.R.A. had tried to make the Tunisian government arrest me. Fortunately, the Tunisian government sensibly refused.

I arrived in Tripoli, and there I realized that no decision had ever been more opportune, as the G.P.R.A. had decided to act against the *Armée de Libération Nationale* and had dismissed its General Staff, Colonel Boumedienne[1] and his two assistants. One of these, Major Slimane, who had been sent on a mission to Constantine, had been arrested and I feared for his life.[2] From Tripoli,

---

[1] I call him 'Colonel Boumedienne' for convenience, as in our interview Ben Bella used a circumlocution, referring to him as the 'present Minister of Defence'.

[2] Slimane was given the Ministry of Tourism, where his administration was criticized by Ben Bella. He later became one of the conspirators of the 19th June. Boumedienne made him his Minister of Finance, an appointment which was 'very variously appreciated' (*Le Monde*).

I immediately issued a statement, in which I indignantly denounced the arbitrary decision of the G.P.R.A.

At the same time, I discovered that the Provisional Government was trying to obtain delivery of a very large consignment of arms, which had been deposited for us in Libya. It was clear that the G.P.R.A. intended these arms for those elements of the *Intérieur* which had been won over by their emissaries. I decided at once to go and see the King of Libya. I went to his house at El-Beïda, outside Benghazi, in the greenest and most enchanting part of Cyrenaica. My friendship with the King was an old one, and in spite of the fact that his government was hostile towards me, I succeeded in persuading him to block the arms.

This was a blow to the G.P.R.A., and there were more to come. They did not manage to persuade the Tunisian government to arrest Colonel Boumedienne. Although he had been 'relieved of his command', he was still in authority over the A.L.N.; the day after the referendum, he crossed the frontier at the head of his troops and marched into Algeria. I believe, although I am unable to prove it, that the G.P.R.A. had asked the French government to close the frontier to the A.L.N., even after the proclamation of Independence.

When I was in Benghazi, I heard that the G.P.R.A. had appointed Belkacem Krim to contact me, accompanied by a very well-known Egyptian, Ali Sabri. Our Egyptian friends were worried about the widening breach in the F.L.N., and begged me to return to Tunis. The G.P.R.A. assured me on their part, through the good offices of Belkacem Krim that, miraculous to relate, I would be very welcome!

Apparently the Egyptians were as sincere as the G.P.R.A. were not, so I decided to go myself and explain everything to Nasser. I took the plane to Cairo, and I told him the whole story. I told him that the G.P.R.A., having wanted to arrest me, only wished for this reconciliation because they felt that I was more dangerous at a distance. I also told him that, as far as I was concerned, I would never go bail for them, because it would mean the end of all my dreams of improving the lot of the people; and that all the intrigues of the G.P.R.A. had only one aim, which was to wring the neck of the Revolution.

It did not take long for Nasser to see that I was in the right. He too had known these 'revolutionaries' who were always talking about 'the people', and whose one idea was to prolong its misery, while retaining their own privileges.

Meanwhile, the referendum took place, and the Independence of Algeria was voted for and proclaimed by a very large majority. The decisive turn had been taken. For me, it was now a question of action; that is to say, of returning to Algeria and denouncing the illegality of the G.P.R.A.

Khider was in Rabat, where he had contacted friendly elements in Morocco itself, and in the Oran district. He wrote to me, saying "The situation is ripe. We are waiting for you." I joined him at once in Rabat. From there, I went to Oujda because, after ten years exile, I wanted to re-enter Algeria by Marnia, my native town.

My welcome in Marnia and Tlemcen, and later in Oran, was marvellous. The sun shone high in the sky, and it was colourful and moving, like an enormous *kermesse*. Those units which had rallied to us drove out to meet us, so that we entered Oran in a caravanserai of several hundred motor-cars, which cruised round the town for hours in the midst of delirious crowds.

After our return, we installed ourselves at first in

Tlemcen, where we began a campaign of explanations. We summoned some groups of our party and some *willaya* representatives and we explained to them what had happened at Tripoli, and how the defeated G.P.R.A. had resigned from the Congress and refused to recognise its validity. After these explanations and the free exchange of views, we published for the first time the details of the Tripoli programme and the composition of the *Bureau Politique*.

From this moment on, our position became very strong. We had at our disposal a Political Bureau (whose members had been correctly elected by the party Congress), a well drawn-up programme of reform, and wide popular support. In addition, the A.L.N., having crossed the Tunisian frontier into Algeria, had established itself in the Constantine, Aurès and Oran districts; in fact, in all the *willayas* which had remained loyal to us.

Meanwhile, the wind of panic blew over the members of the G.P.R.A., who realised that they had lost the game and gave in, with the exception of Boudiaf and Belkacem Krim. These two tried to launch a resistance movement based on Kabyle separatism.

That this separatism exists cannot be denied; but it is really nothing more than a legacy of colonialism. The French administration had always tried to play off the Kabyles against the Arabs. It had never succeeded, however, in giving a definite political character to this regionalism. Proof of this lay in the fact that, when the right moment came, Kabylia enthusiastically joined the Algerian Revolution and provided it with some of its most valuable elements. The attempt of Boudiaf and Krim Belkacem in Kabylia was rapidly checked; but nevertheless it contained the germs of a potential danger.

No sooner had it been installed in Algiers than the *Bureau Politique* found itself up against a far more dangerous enemy than the G.P.R.A. I have already explained how the *willayas*, through lack of a really centralized executive policy and having been abandoned by the *Extérieur*, had appropriated areas of countryside over which they ruled as masters, and which they intended to keep. The five members of the *Bureau Politique* had hardly arrived in Algiers before they found themselves, so to speak, enclosed in a world which baffled them. Their power was only nominal; real power lay in the hands of the IVth *willaya*, which had set itself up as a state and which was in control of the armed forces, the radio station, and certain administrative bodies.

In addition, in order to defend themselves against attacks by 'local forces' and the O.A.S., the *willayas* had enormously increased in size after the Evian agreements. Alongside the genuine fighters, many doubtful and unruly elements had been recruited. These elements were responsible for the extortions and crimes committed against Europeans at this period. The wife of the Swedish consul was raped in the presence of her husband; the Italian consul's car was machine-gunned; two Belgians had their throats cut in the forest of Baïnem; and French school-teachers had been massacred.

We had got to put a stop to this anarchy. I insisted that the IVth *willaya* should evacuate Algiers and surrender the instruments of power. It refused. The *Bureau Politique* published a communiqué denouncing its attitude. The IVth *willaya* answered with a communiqué attacking our position; the war of communiqués continued for several days. But it was clear that by prolonging this situation, we would only make things go from bad to worse. So the *Bureau Politique* decided to call upon the

A.L.N. to march on Algiers, and force the IVth *willaya* to respond to reason. Unfortunately, the *willaya* did not give in at once; there was a clash of arms, and blood was shed.

I took care that at least there should be no bloodshed in Kabylia, as I wanted to be sure that there could not later be any exploitation of the separatism which I have described, which could raise difficulties for the Algerian government. Certain Kabyle groups had, against our orders, occupied Bougie, which formed part of the IIIrd *willaya*. At my request, the A.L.N. refrained from intervention: I myself went to see the Kabyles and persuaded them to accept a compromise, whereby order was restored without loss of face.

At the time when I had to tackle all these problems, I had already moved into the Villa Joly. Since then, I have never wanted to leave it, as its walls remind me so strongly of those first days of my return to Algiers. At night I slept for barely three hours, with the most incredible din going on around me. The building was, in fact, my headquarters and there were about a hundred of us there all the time, sleeping as best we could in the empty rooms and eating or not eating, as best we might.

The morning after my first night in the Villa Joly, I could not find anyone in the whole building to cook breakfast. So I got someone to take me to the nearest café, where I asked for a *café crème*. It was early and I was the only person standing at the counter, when the French *patronne* came up to me and said "Monsieur, are you not Ben Bella?" "Yes, madame," I answered, "I am." While I was drinking my coffee, I started chatting to her. She listened to me silently, answering with nods of her head, with a look of utter amazement. Obviously, the press and the radio had produced an apocalyptic vision of me and she was finding it impossible to reconcile this image with the reality of the man standing in front of her. There I was, alone and unarmed, standing at her counter talking politely to her and apparently enjoying her coffee. And, like anyone else, I was stirring the spoon round and round the cup to make the sugar melt!

The Villa Joly had been abandoned by French government officials at the moment when the *Bureau Politique* was planning its return to Algiers, and it had been found for me by Khemisti. At all costs, I wanted to avoid installing myself in the Palais d'Eté, whose ostentation seemed to me incompatible with the spirit of the Revolution. Poor Khemisti,[1] incidentally, had been Farès' *directeur du cabinet* in the *Exécutif Provisoire*. It was through him that we had been kept in almost hourly touch with the internal movements of this body, of whom we had some reason to feel suspicious.

The defeat and subjection of the IVth *willaya* had by no means sounded the death-knell of *willayisme*. Although the big towns were fairly safe, the countryside was still overrun by unruly elements armed with machine guns, who practised the most odious extortions under cover of patriotism. I had to be constantly on the alert and was continually taking action against them: at Maison Blanche, where a gang had attacked some *colons*, and at Marengo, where a farm was being held up to ransom. I had to send out detachments of the A.L.N., as it was our only police force at that time; but these gangsters thought that they could do as they liked, and our men were sometimes fired at. Here and there, we encountered serious difficulties and delays, and it was several months before we finally cleared up the aftermath of *willayisme*.

[1] When Ben Bella formed his government, Khemisti became one of the youngest ministers of foreign affairs in the world. A few months later he was murdered by a fanatic.

When Independence was declared, the Algerian state was still only a fiction, a *Bureau Politique* composed of five men; now, it was slowly becoming a reality in spite of innumerable difficulties. On the 15th September, general elections took place throughout Algeria. On the 27th, my government was formed; and on the 3rd October, I left for the United Nations.

It was a very moving moment for us when the Algerian flag was hoisted for the first time, and went up into the sky to unfurl itself among those of the other U.N.O. countries. Sekou Touré had been good enough to make the long journey from Africa to America in order to be present at the ceremony, and I was very touched to have him standing beside me.

Everyone expected my speech to U.N.O. to be a shattering one, but instead it was moderate in tone, though firm in its intentions. I did not attack France because, from now on, we intended to live side by side on good terms, as was implicit in the very nature of things.

We had to give a reception in honour of our admission to U.N.O., and I remember that our friends accordingly advised me to get in supplies of gin and whisky and other drinks for our guests. "One has to do it," they told me. "It is the custom here, even the Arab countries conform." "Even if it is the custom," I said, "I am not going to do it. Algeria is a Moslem country. She will offer hospitality according to her own traditions, not other people's." "It will be a complete fiasco!" they groaned. "The Americans will not come." "If they are our friends, they will come," I answered. And they came—they even came in crowds, and for two hours they bravely quenched their thirst with orange-juice.

Meanwhile, the American press let fly against me.

There were two reasons for their anger: one was my position regarding the question of Israel, and the other was my attitude towards Cuba.

I had never doubted that Israel was the bridgehead of western imperialism in the Middle East, and I had said so again and again. This was good enough reason for hordes of journalists to either hint accusingly at anti-semitism, or to express veiled hatred of me without giving any reason. I indignantly reject the accusation of anti-semitism; it is pure calumny. I am not, never have been, and never will be a racialist. Because I have denounced the sinister part played by Israel in the heart of the Arab world, my accusers pretend to believe that I am anti-semitic: but it is they who are guilty of racialism.

During the Algerian war, a number of progressive journalists in France had gravitated round the miracle-working G.P.R.A., and had blindly taken its side against me at the time of our Independence. As most of these journalists were Jews, their prejudice against me was nourished by their secret Zionist sympathies. I said as much to some of them when they were good enough to come and see me in Algiers. "You progressives, you anti-racialists—what do you think you are attacking when you make these angry accusations against me? You are attacking an anti-racialist government which is trying to establish socialism. We want a true revolution: the G.P.R.A. did not. The G.P.R.A. thought that, by drinking alcohol with their European friends, they were being 'democratic', 'socialist', and 'advanced'. By denigrating us, you are denigrating the only effective progressive force in this country. And you do harm to the Israeli cause in the world, because you are confusing it with the doubtful and contestable cause of Zionism."

Nobody is going to make me believe that the role of

Israel in Africa is a progressive one. On the contrary, there is a kind of tacit understanding between Israel and western imperialism for Israel to take over, or endeavour to take over, those positions in Africa which the West has been forced to abandon. Thus, at the moment, seventy-five per cent of Israel's trade is with South Africa, which makes one wonder slightly, when one considers the odious racialist policy of that country.

To return to the United States and its press outburst against me. Before going to the United Nations, I had received an invitation to go and see President Kennedy. Before this, I had also received one from Castro. The problem raised by these two invitations was discussed at our cabinet meeting. On consideration, it seemed impossible for us to go to Washington without afterwards going to Cuba, both from the political and from the purely friendly points of view. Even before leaving Algiers, we informed the Americans accordingly. Their reaction was very sharp. They did not actually say so but, reading between the lines of their answer, one could easily guess that they wanted to say: As you are going to Cuba, it is no use coming to see us. Of course their reaction was well wrapped up in the usual unctuous diplomatic language. But in America, when the press discovered that I was going to meet Castro after having been received by Kennedy, it became hysterical. I was treated worse than the devil in all the newspaper offices of America.

The atmosphere remained tense, even in official circles: when Kennedy gave a reception in honour of Algeria, it was almost a disaster. I was told that I would have to be introduced to the *Corps Diplomatique* by the South-Vietnamese representative, as he was the *doyen*. I immediately protested. "I do not recognize the government of South Vietnam," I told the Americans, "I do not there-

fore wish to shake this gentleman by the hand, and even
less do I wish to be introduced by him to anyone." The
discussion became heated, but the Americans finally gave
way. At the reception, the South-Vietnamese representative came towards me, but I pointedly turned away. He
had doubtless been warned by his employers, as he
walked past me without stopping. Far from introducing
me to his colleagues, he had not even dared to introduce
himself!

I liked Kennedy even before I had met him because I
knew that, as long ago as 1957, he had made a speech
calling for Algerian independence. He invited me to
lunch, and I was not disappointed by his approach. He
gave me the impression of a courageous and honest man,
but he seemed to be subjected to endless pressure and to
be, to an extraordinary degree, the prisoner of a system.
When I told him that I deplored the fact that American
foreign policy supported corrupt régimes in the world and
attacked disinterested leaders like Castro and Nasser, I
have to admit that his answer did not seem to me very
convincing.

On the subject of Cuba he told me that, if need be, he
could accept Communism in that large island, provided
that it was of the Yugoslavian or Polish variety; but that
he could not accept 'expansionist' Communism, which
would spread revolution throughout South America. He
also told me that he could never agree to allow a missile
base on the island. While we were on this subject, I could
not help remarking on the fact that Cuba had been forced
to allow an American military base on her own territory.

Our conversation was very lively and, on both sides,
extremely frank. I remember that I said to him at one
moment, quite vehemently: "Why do you persecute
Castro? Why persist in this cruel blockade? I warn you,

that if you do the same to us, you will have a second Cuba in Africa."

I finally took my leave of Kennedy with personal feelings of sympathy and respect towards him, but without many illusions about the State Department's policy towards us, nor about their promise of financial support for us which was, in fact, very soon to be forgotten. Kennedy seemed to represent the moderate element, in opposition to the bellicose policy of his country. I felt that his death was a great loss for the U.S.A. and for the whole world. I remember that I was sitting in my room in the Villa Joly, when the telegram came with the news that he had been shot in Dallas. I had hardly finished reading it when a second message came, to say that he was dead. I leapt to my feet, staggered by the news. Without waiting to summon my cabinet, I telephoned at once to the radio station. I dictated a statement in which I immediately denounced the racialist and police-organized machinations of which Kennedy had been the victim, and which would now, naturally, be attributed to Fidel Castro.

A few days later, I named the big square at El-Biar in memory of President Kennedy.

When the moment came for me to leave the United States, it was only with great difficulty that the Americans were persuaded to allow a Cuban plane to come and fetch me. Their attitude was so hostile that at one point I was afraid that the C.I.A., without the President's knowledge, would sabotage the plane at the airport or have it attacked in mid-air by anti-Castro airmen in its service. However, as soon as we set foot in the plane, the Cubans threw themselves into our arms and we soon forgot our fears.

In the United States, I had missed the warmth of human relations more than anything else. America is like

5*

a wall: right from the start, those vertical cities with their enormous buildings gave me this impression. What is missing is communication from man to man. Although those great American cities are like ant-heaps full of men, they are also like deserts. I had never seen so many people as I saw in America, but I had never felt so much alone. In those crowds of human beings, there was an inhuman emptiness; there was a complete absence of human emotions, which to us Algerians are an essential part of life, without which we are unable to breathe.

We were all the more delighted to bask in the warmth of Cuban friendliness which greeted us in the plane. We had hardly taken our seats before they produced excellent *cafecito*, very strong and sweet and aromatic, which was a welcome change after the insipid brew which is called coffee in the United States. We all started talking at once in no known language, as they could talk no Arabic and I knew very little Spanish. Friendliness made up for everything.

The Algerians rightly claim kinship with the Arab world, in which they never feel that they are foreigners. In Cairo, Baghdad or Damascus, in spite of considerable differences, we always find something which suddenly reminds us that we are at home—the look of a street, a word or a gesture, or some shared custom. The Cubans are a much more exuberant people than us, and we have nothing in common; neither race, customs, language, nor even character. But strangely enough, communication between Algerians and Cubans is instantaneous, and deeply felt.

Fidel was waiting to meet us at Havana airport with his ministers and all his government: they all felt deeply moved, and were filled with brotherly love, and were overjoyed to see us. I had taken great trouble to prepare my speech in Spanish, but I was so overcome with emotion that I made many mistakes and delivered it very badly. My audience could not have cared less, and they cheered me after each sentence. The tropical autumn sun made the hot air literally dance around us, and the Cuban crowds were filled with fervour, energy, and vitality.

As soon as I had finished my speech, Fidel came up and gave me a *fuerte abrazo*[1] and waves of applause rang out again and again. I could see a group of Algerian children coming towards me; they were the sons of *chouhadas*,[2] who had been the guests of Fidel for two years. I was terribly moved to see them there. I was told that they had worked very hard and could now speak perfect Spanish. They had played for their group in the finals of the Cuban University football match, but they had lost the match through disqualification. They had behaved like true Algerians—they had come to blows with their opponents!

We only stayed thirty-six hours in Cuba, but those thirty-six hours were one long *fiesta*! A programme had been drawn up by someone, but whoever it was, Fidel took no notice, and protocol was turned upside down while we talked, and talked, and talked. The two youngest revolutions in the world were meeting for the first time and comparing their problems. Together, we built our future.

The day after our arrival, Fidel took us to see the beach of Varadero. He showed us a nationalized farm, and a valley which he had replanted with trees. I admired the Cuban leader for not allowing the most serious worries to affect his sense of humour. He had ordered an escort of

---

[1] A hearty embrace.
[2] These children had been rescued by Fidel Castro from Oran in 1960, and taken to Cuba via Morocco. There were thirty of them, accompanied by a school-teacher called Ben Smaïl.

motor-cycle outriders in our honour. They were dressed
in scarlet, like jockeys, and were meant to drive in front
of our car; in fact, we frequently had to stop and wait for
them, as they invariably took the wrong turn at every
cross-road. Finally, Fidel became impatient and jumped
out of the car: I expected him to rebuke them. The
rebuke was delivered, but in a totally unexpected way.
"Look here, *compañeros,*" said Fidel, "are we going to see
this farm, or are we not? Do I know this farm, or do I
not? And does this farm even exist? You have managed
to make me wonder if we are even in Cuba." Whereupon
everyone, including the outriders, burst out laughing and
Fidel got back into the car.

Fidel was worried about the state of our defences. "I
know that you have a very good army," he said, "but
have you any tanks?" "No, at present we have none."
He remembered this conversation several months later,
at the time of our frontier war with Morocco. We had
ordered a cargo of sugar from Cuba; he sent the cargo
and, when our dockers were unloading it, they found
tanks hidden in the sugar.

I spoke to him of our agricultural problems. I told him
that we, as Moslems, do not drink wine and that perhaps
we ought to scrap the vineyards. He said: "No, no, don't
do that. We made the same mistake ourselves in the
beginning, over sugar-cane. Vineyards are the best thing
colonialism gave you, so keep them: and plant more of
them. Your wine has a very high alcohol content and you
will always be able to sell it."

Thirty-six hours had never passed so quickly, and we
felt extraordinarily sad at leaving Fidel. We invited him
to come to Algeria; but would he ever be able to? The
threat of war was hanging over Cuba night and day, as
though it were dangling on the end of a thread.

When we landed at Algiers airport, my heart began to beat at the sight of the great town, spread like a crescent along the shores of its bay. This wonderful country had been at war for seven years, and had lost a million dead; it was still scarred and bleeding, and its people were poverty-stricken. It had got to be rebuilt, on new foundations, from top to bottom. Would fate allow me the time in which to do it?

7

First Problems

The situation in Algeria, after seven years of war, was appalling. The country had been bled dry, and everything was dislocated. The O.A.S. had blown up schools with plastic bombs, burnt down the library of Algiers University, and destroyed tons of administrative files. Thousands of teachers had abandoned their posts. The French army, on the other hand, still occupied the country according to the Evian agreements, and we still depended closely on the French government for a lot of things. Then again, the massive exodus of nine-tenths of the French population of Algeria in the summer of 1962 had brought about a collapse of the economic structure. Out of ten million Algerians, there were two million unemployed, including over two hundred and fifty thousand in the town of Algiers alone. Urban unemployment had been aggravated by an influx of starving people from the country districts. I had already observed this phenomenon at Marnia after the Second World War, but this time the numbers were far greater, and it lasted longer than in 1945.

What did the *fellah* hope to find in Algiers, Oran and Constantine during that summer of 1962? The answer is food, schools for his children, medical assistance for himself and his family, and also cheap housing. For the *fellah* knew that crowds of impoverished townspeople, in an overwhelming rush, had seized many of the houses which had been abandoned by the French in the exodus.[1] The problem of this army of urban unemployed was well-nigh insoluble; there was not, and there would not be for a very long time, enough industry to absorb them. It was therefore necessary to try and convince them that they must return to the land. Before all else, we had to re-organize the agricultural sector, both to provide the un-employed with work, and to ensure the country's food supplies. 'Operation Ploughing' was therefore our first battle.

The operation was launched on the 15th September, and after a month and a half it suffered a grave setback. We had made a serious mistake, and the situation was critical. The socialist countries had promised to send us tractors, and the press and radio had already announced their arrival. In the minds of the *fellaheen* this meant that other people were coming to do the ploughing for them: consequently, nobody did any more work. Nobody in the local administration took even the smallest initiative; everyone was waiting for the tractors.

I decided to adopt radical methods. I summoned a meeting of the S.A.P.[2] in Algiers, thereby going over the heads of *préfets*, *sous-préfets*, and mayors. I explained to them that we had just got to roll up our shirt-sleeves and start ploughing with anything which was available. Once we had decided in principle, a thousand questions of

---

[1] 'Recovery' by individuals of reputedly abandoned houses (which had, in fact, usually been left locked up by their owners), is a procedure which has nothing to do with the nationalization of private industrial property, which socialism means to introduce. Unfortunately, it is only too true that neither the *Exécutif Provisoire* nor the *Bureau Politique* was in a position, at that time, to curb or prevent this abnormal situation. On the other hand, the Algerian government once established could not go back on this '*fait accompli*' without alienating the majority of the urban population. The whole case of 'unclaimed property' is very weak legally, and it was only used as an excuse after the event to justify expropriations, which the French government would have been well advised to treat as 'war damage' from the start, no matter what financial situation might have resulted.

[2] *Société Agricole de Prévoyance.*

detail arose, which I had to answer from one day to the next for two months. Whenever a breakdown was reported to me, I would rush off to the site and investigate: if the need arose, I would penalize the incompetent administrator, without going through the formality of advising my Minister of the Interior. I requisitioned seed, ploughs, and tractors on the spot. These were unorthodox methods which were censured by some people, who could only shout "Dictatorship!" But which was preferable, to respect the formalities and lose the battle of 'Operation Ploughing', or to disregard them and win it?

In the end, we won it. The ploughing and sowing were finished within our time limit; in addition, the rains were favourable, and in 1963 we had a magnificent harvest.

In the autumn my government took a decision which caused a great deal of ink to flow: it put the Algerian Communist Party under an interdiction. This measure, as a matter of fact, was somewhat badly presented to the public and, because it was never adequately explained, it made us appear to be in the anti-communist camp. In fact, the decision occurred in a historical context which shows the true meaning of this act.

We had fought so hard and made so many sacrifices to preserve the unity of the F.L.N., both before and after the 1st November (because we felt that this unity was essential to its strength and its future success), that I must admit that we had never even considered the possibility of allowing a crop of political parties to mature in Algeria, once we were in power. In actual fact, after the Declaration of Independence, we purposely excluded this possibility in the Tripoli programme, as to us it seemed like a 'luxury' which an underdeveloped country could not permit itself.

Underdeveloped countries are, indeed, extremely vulnerable. Most of them exist solely by the production of some one kind of agricultural raw material: in Cuba, for instance, it is sugar. In certain African countries it is coffee; it is wine in Algeria, jute in Pakistan, and cotton in Egypt. Now, the price of these raw materials is fixed, not in the capital city where they are sold, but in the capitals of the West, where they are bought. It follows that the underdeveloped countries are always dependent, always tributary, always exploited, and the disparity between their standard of living and that of the great industrial countries, far from becoming smaller with the passage of time, is merely aggravated. The great nations can ease their consciences by allowing two, three, or many more political parties: it is flattering to them and creates a good impression. The more so as, in the countries of the West, once they are in power both socialists and conservatives serve the interests of imperialism with equal docility. But we are still an impoverished and illiterate people, whose average earning capacity is nowhere more than twenty thousand old francs a year,[1] and we are not strong enough to allow ourselves to play such a sophisticated game. In our country, it could only lead to confusion, division, and anarchy; or even worse, to the surreptitious and unwarrantable interference by a foreign power in the fight for votes. We needed a single party which could unite and lead all the country's different elements: a party which could act, and act quickly, to make up for lost time in the reorganization of the social and economic structure from top to bottom.

The Algerian Communist Party had taken part in the fight for national liberation—but in what capacity? It had not joined the movement as a party, but had allowed

[1] Tr. note: about £15.10.0.

certain of its elements to become integrated with the
F.L.N. Now that peace had returned, could we allow
these elements to break away from us and re-establish
the Algerian Communist Party? And if we allowed this,
why should we not also allow Monsieur Ferhat Abbas to
resuscitate the U.D.M.A.? One can see, or feel, or guess
the dangers to which this policy would have exposed us.

There were different reactions to our decision in the
outside world. Some rejoiced prematurely, others grieved
without cause. For a time, the socialist leaders treated us
with a certain coldness, with the exception of Fidel
Castro, to whom I had written immediately, explaining
the full significance of the decree. During the month
which followed, I carried on with this clarification of our
policy. I explained my point of view very thoroughly to
the Italian communists, whom I found particularly intelligent and open-minded during the interview which I
gave them. Next, I took good care to reaffirm the strong
intention of my government not to be trapped in the
gilded snare of anti-communism. A little later, I declared
in public that if the Soviet Union had not existed, we
would have had to invent it, if only to play a trick on the
devouring expansionism of imperialism.

I must add that, from the humanitarian point of view,
I feel great respect for militant communists. I admire
them for being so detached from the small petty world of
personal interests. Money, success, and a career do not
seem to count for them. They are ready to sacrifice everything at a moment's notice for the sake of their political
ideals, including their liberty and their lives. I feel very
close to them on this score.

I also admit the force of their economic reasoning. I
only part company with them over their philosophical
beliefs: they are atheists, and I believe in God. Of course,

I know well that I cannot prove my religious beliefs, and that they must remain in the world of conjecture. Nevertheless, these beliefs are deep within me and I am strongly attached to them, although without fanaticism or narrowness. Besides, I cannot see why a believer, be he Moslem or Christian, cannot agree with a militant communist in the field of material planning. I am talking of a true believer and not of one of those clever people who use their 'faith' to defend and sanctify retrograde social theories.

I place education at the top of those causes which were, and still are, closest to our hearts. The reopening of the school term in October 1962 brought with it some terrible problems, as I have already said. It must be admitted that finally they were largely solved by the school-masters and professors of the *Coopération*,[1] who answered the appeal of the French government in large numbers. On our part, we were very much aware of what was at stake—the speedy training of personnel, of whom the country was in urgent need—so we therefore decided to make a prodigious effort. Algeria is one of the few countries which devotes a quarter of its budget to education, a fact which is perhaps not sufficiently appreciated, either here or on the other side of the Mediterranean.

The opening of term at Algiers University was celebrated with special solemnity, as much to pay public tribute to the eminent French teachers among us as to emphasize the enormous importance which we attach to education. I decided to take part in the ceremony, and I gave an address in which I set out some of the opinions in which I believe. Over the years, we have lost the use of the noble language of our ancestors, and in losing it we

[1] Tr. note: after the Evian agreements, one of the duties of the French government to the Algerian Republic was to send a certain number of teachers and technicians to help the new state. These were all volunteers.

have also lost our moral and intellectual standing; my speech seemed a good occasion on which to emphasize the importance of regaining this standing, while at the same time affirming our respect for French culture.

It is very noticeable that, when the colonial learns a foreign language, he more or less adopts the mental attitudes which that language interprets. If he still possesses and utilizes his own language, his experience will be enriched by this process. But if his thoughts are no longer inspired by his own language, and have to be conveyed in the speech of the conqueror, then it is clear that there is real estrangement from his native tongue. This estrangement was accepted and even welcomed by certain of our Algerian intellectuals who, without admitting it, felt themselves to be essentially more French than Algerian. This was the result of snobbery, opportunism, and a lack of political judgement; it was also because they were fascinated by the world prestige of the French language. As for the Arabic language, all they could feel towards it was a sense of remoteness.

I consider that an attitude of this kind is very harmful, because it implies a process of de-nationalization in the minds of those Algerian intellectuals who give way to it. It would be dangerous if compulsory education were to spread this outlook throughout the framework of the future state.

Algerians such as myself who do not accept this estrangement from the Arabic language, nevertheless notice it in the deep disquiet which they experience when they try to give expression to their ideas in French, while at the same time they 'feel' in Arabic. A state of perpetual divorce is thus established in us, between the head and the heart, and between the intellect and the emotions.

It would certainly be folly to declare war on the French

language in the name of ill-conceived nationalism, because it provides a most necessary bridge between the
Algerian intelligentsia and Western expert knowledge.
On the contrary, as we have acquired it, we must preserve
that breadth of mind which the French language has
given us. But at the same time we must recover that
other language which we have lost, and that richness
which we Arabs ought to derive from the Arabic language. We must, however, face up to the fact that this is
a long-term proposition, which will take fifteen or twenty
years to materialize.[1]

The *Petits Cireurs* operation took place in February
1963. The sight of swarms of thin and ragged children on
their knees at the feet of healthy adults, removing the
filth from their boots, had always seemed to me symbolic
of the humiliation of the 'natives' in underdeveloped
countries. And I was by no means the only one who considered it to be scandalous. Since the formation of my
government, I received letters every day from Algerian
men and women, saying: "Our President, we are suffering
from poverty and hunger. But our greatest unhappiness
is to see these children in the streets, polishing the shoes
of the foreigners, and even sometimes those of Algerians.
This is a disgrace, our President; it is an assault on our
dignity, and we ought not to allow it."

I know exactly what the answer to those letters
would have been from a theoretical socialist: the only
practical solution to the problem of the shoe-shine boys
is an economic one. Abolish unemployment, and the

---

[1] The language problem has, in fact, greatly complicated the task of the Algerian
schoolboy. At school he learns classical Arabic; at home he speaks Arab dialect; and
ultimately he has to learn certain subjects in French. On the other hand, it has proved
almost impossible from a practical point of view, to choose once and for all between
French and Arabic. This has put a considerable brake on the efforts of Ben Bella's
government to combat illiteracy.

exploitation of children will cease automatically. Suppress the cause, and the effect will disappear.

That is the orthodox answer which, though economically correct, is not acceptable in terms of human beings. It would take years to eradicate the cause, and meanwhile the shoe-shine boys would be abandoned to filth and disease, illiteracy and humiliation. The more I pondered the question, the more I was convinced that I could not sacrifice those thousands of children by postponing the solution of their problem.

I therefore resigned myself to doing that which all good economists condemn: I decided to attack the effect rather than the cause. I discussed the means at our disposal with Boumaza.[1] We decided to assemble the shoe-shine boys in the Salle Ibn Khaldoun and, after explaining our plan to them, to distribute them among different rehabilitation centres. The operation was carried out amid the delirious enthusiasm of the Algerian people, and was a very great success.

Of course there were people among us who declared that these children were too degraded, after so many years of misery, lawlessness and filth, to be able to earn anything at all. Pessimism is often a mask, behind which the spirit of reaction hides: I was not taken in by this way of thinking. At my request, the teachers in charge of the shoe-shine boys made a preliminary experiment. They selected four children from among those whom they considered to be the most intelligent, who had had some teaching in the past but had been obliged to give it up. They were now given a concentrated course, and after three months they sat for the entrance examination of a lycée. All four of them passed. Encouraged by this experi-

---

[1] Ben Bella's Minister of Economic Affairs, who sided with Boumedienne after the coup d'état of the 19th June, 1965.

ment, fifty boys from Bône were then chosen and, after two months' hard work, they reached the standard required for the entrance examination of a technical school. Thus, the prophecies of the pessimists were once again proved false.

There were still some shoe-cleaners to be seen a few months later, in Bresson Square in Algiers; but this time they were adults, either hunchbacks, or cripples, or deformities. We let them carry on for the time being, while making the reservation that we would also deal with them in due course. For there can be no question of tolerating the renewal of such a degrading profession in free Algeria. Arrogant and lazy people will have to do as I do: buy a brush, and clean their own shoes.

The framework of our welfare campaign also included the provision of homes for old men, the '*Bouchée de Pain*' for women, and a home for elderly couples at Sidi-Moussa. At the time when my government was formed, there were hundreds and hundreds of old men and women sleeping under the arcades of Algiers. I was working until very late at night at that time, and before going to bed between one and two in the morning, I used always to be driven round the town to get some fresh air. Human shapes lay stretched out everywhere, motionless, and wrapped in rags. In the shadows of the arcades they looked like the corpses of people who had dropped dead in the struggle for life, and night after night my heart ached to see them in such numbers. It was a happy day for me when, after having opened the various centres which I have mentioned, the order went out to collect these poor wretches and settle them in the homes which awaited them.

We carried out these operations because, quite simply,

they satisfied one of the deeply-felt longings of the Algerian people; but we were fully aware that the essential problem still remained to be solved. Our people had just emerged from a hundred and thirty years of darkness and neglect; they needed to have visible and tangible proof that the Algerian authorities were really working for their good. They expected affection and care from the first Algerian government of Algeria, like a child who wakes up after a nightmare and needs consoling and caressing.

I had never appreciated this state of mind so fully as when I was going my rounds by car. I was driving through a small village one day when I found the *fellaheen* building a mosque, so I decided to stop, and I got out of the car. I was recognized at once and immediately surrounded by village people. We had started talking, when an old man came up to me and said: "Ahmed! At last you have come! But you have been too long coming to see us—why have you been such a long time? You have been President for months now, and we have been waiting and waiting for you." I said to him: "My father, Algeria is a big country, and there are over a thousand large villages. Even if I visited three a day every day of the year, and did nothing else, it would take me over a year. So just think what a long time it would take me to visit twenty thousand small villages such as yours." "Yes, yes," said the old man, "you are right, Ahmed. Nevertheless, we have been waiting and waiting." And the crowd around him agreed with what he had said.

It was because I could feel the pulse of the people that I knew that immediate action was needed to stop abuse. It was necessary to use somewhat unorthodox, or quite simply, revolutionary methods. The prices of meat and vegetables suddenly started to soar during January and February 1963, at the time of *Ramadan*. I instituted an inquiry, and discovered that these cruel and abusive rises in price were the work of the market middlemen. These are the people who, in a capitalist economy, are far more powerful than the President of a Republic; they can control the most efficient government apparatus by sheer trickery.

The war, Revolution, and Independence had passed these gentlemen by without leaving a mark on them. Having lent money to the farmers to finance the planting of certain vegetables, they were in control of the crops, which were thus already mortgaged to them. This enabled them to sit at their telephones and gamble (on a certainty) on the rising prices. They would telephone to the growers, saying: "Do not bring any tomatoes today." Then there would be a tomato shortage, the price would rise, and when it had reached the desired level, the middlemen would once more open the flood-gates.

They achieved the same results by an even simpler procedure, that of 'stocking'. Instead of distributing a certain vegetable in the market, they would keep back stocks of it. One day, I went down to the market myself, summoned the middlemen and said to them: "I am told that there are no more onions in the market. But I have just seen quantities of them in your stores." "Mr. President," they said, smiling politely, "we cannot touch those, they are for stocking." "For stocking?" I asked. "What does that mean?" "It means, Mr. President, that they are sold." Perfectly correct bills were at once produced, signed by non-existent men. "Very good," I said, "everything is in order." They smiled to each other as they watched me leaving.

But the next day the smiles disappeared, when I returned at the head of a crowd of two thousand children. I showed them the famous 'stocks' of onions, and said to them: "Get going! Today, everything is free. Now is the moment to replenish the larders of your families." Then the children flung themselves on the stocks of onions: wherever they had passed, there was no longer an onion to be seen. As I left, I said to these gentlemen: "I'll be back tomorrow with four thousand children." But it was not necessary; they had realized that the splendid game of 'stocking' could no longer be played in the new Algeria.

The wholesale butchers are to meat what the middle-men are to vegetables. But if I may venture to say so, they are even more close-fisted, and all measures against them failed, except force. We had to put all of them in prison: I repeat, all of them. They were thunderstruck that anyone had dared to treat them like this, as they had numerous accomplices and backers and had up to now felt quite safe, thanks to their ill-gotten millions. One of the leaders of the moderate nationalist party came to see me, looking very offended. "What is this?" he said to me. "You have put Hedroug in prison? But he is a very good man, and what's more, he is my friend." Needless to say I knew that Hedroug was his friend and 'what's more' a very generous one, as he had given him the villa he was living in. My visitor was politely bowed out, and Hedroug remained in prison.

The condition of the *fellah* had worried me for a long time. I drove all through the Mitidja during *Ramadan*, and I was sickened by the sight of miserable mud houses alongside the magnificent villas of the *colons*. I stopped outside one of these hovels, and said to an elderly man: "Are you all right, my father?" He recognized me and got up, taking my hand and saying: "How can I be all right, when the *colon*" (with here a string of insults) "houses me and my family worse than he does his

animals? Come, my son, come: I will show you the house
he has given me." It was indeed horrifying: a single
small room with a leaking roof, and marks on the walls
where the rain had streamed down. "I have lived here
for forty years," said the man, "I had seven children: all
seven died of tuberculosis. Here is the eighth." His wife
was sitting on the floor in a corner of the room, a puny
child in her arms. I left the room, appalled. "Where is
your master?" I said. "He is in France." "Well then,
where is his manager?" "At Boufarik." "Get into the car
with me. I want to talk to him." At Boufarik, seventeen
kilometres away, I found the manager sitting in a café
drinking an apéritif. I made him come outside, and said
to him: "Listen to me. I am not going to lecture you,
because it would be of no use. But I can tell you this: if
this old man is not given a better house in two months, I
shall deal with you." Thereupon I turned on my heels.
Then I drove the old man home.

This episode helped me to put my finger on the paradoxical and intolerable situation which was general in
Algeria at that time. Political power was in the hands of
the Algerians; but economic power, including the land
itself, was still in the hands of Europeans. They were still
in possession of their vast estates and they continued to
exploit the *fellah*, as in the past. It was clear that this
state of affairs was contrary to even the most elementary
ideas of justice. As long as Algerian soil was still in the
hands of the big landowners, whether French or Algerian,
the words 'Independence' and 'Revolution' made no sense,
and the Tripoli programme remained a dead letter.

In March 1963, my government promulgated the decree
nationalizing the majority of the big landed properties.
Some of the *colons*, at the time of the Evian agreements,
had sabotaged their machinery, burnt their harvests, and

destroyed their stocks before leaving the country. As there was now some anxiety that the big estates might be sabotaged by their dispossessed owners, it was decided to take possession of them before the decree was made public. The A.N.P.,[1] in a remarkably secret and well-organized manner, marched on the big estates very early one morning and occupied them, calling upon their owners to leave. This is how Borgeaud's famous 'La Trappe' was nationalized, also the properties owned by Germain, Aversenq, and Gratien Faure.

There was an outburst of joy throughout the whole country, and I must confess that I had never felt so happy in all my life. The land had come back to the people who cultivated it and Algeria had taken a decisive step on the road to socialism. There were, of course, some reactions from the French government; they were fairly strong ones, but not enough to provoke a real crisis in the relations between the two countries. I was told that Borgeaud, whose name symbolized French colonialism to the Algerian people, was 'very surprised' by the blow which had struck him. He immediately left for France where, presumably, every comfort awaited him. I visited La Trappe, with its famous motto,[2] after his departure. The house was so astonishing, and so typical, that I decided that not a stick of furniture, not a book, not an ornament was to be moved. My intention is to preserve Borgeaud's house just as he left it, and to turn it into a museum where future generations of Algerians will be able to see how the great feudal lords lived, in the days when we were their serfs.

We had not been able to nationalize everything, far

---

[1] After the Declaration of Independence, the A.L.N. (*Armée de Libération Nationale*) became the A.N.P., or *Armée Nationale Populaire*.
[2] "By the sword, the cross, and the plough."

from it, and every day I received hundreds of letters bringing to my notice properties which we had over-looked. One day I was driving through a small village called En Aïa, not far from Marnia; my car had just managed to get clear of the crowds, when I saw a man of about thirty running alongside, shouting to me and brandishing a piece of paper. He was running at a crazy speed and had almost caught up with the car; as he ran, he tried to show me his piece of paper and shouted something to me. I told the chauffeur to slow down, opened the window, and made a friendly gesture to the man with my hand. I finally managed to hear what he was saying. He was shouting at the top of his voice: "Grasset! Grasset!" But I was none the wiser, and nobody around me was able to enlighten me.

I put the question to the *préfet* that evening: he started to laugh. "Yvon Grasset is a big landowner in these parts. Your runner was trying to tell you that his farm has not yet been nationalized." I asked: "Is it a big farm?" "Nearly a thousand acres of good land." "Listen to me," I said, "this is scandalous. You will please nationalize it from tomorrow." And then a moment later, I remembered my runner of that morning and was greatly cheered by the thought of the joy he would feel on hearing of my decision. There could never have been a better prize for the hundred yards!

This man, Grasset, incidentally, had been my fellow-student at Tlemcen. I had played football against him and I remembered that, as a man, I had always liked him. But needless to say, he had to suffer the common fate; I could make no exceptions, neither for him, nor for any of my compatriots.

There was great danger that the richest of the Al-gerians would replace the French propertied classes and constitute an autochthonous middle class, which would continue to keep the masses in a state of poverty. After the Evian agreements, a certain number of properties, both in the towns and in the country, had passed from the hands of Europeans into those of Algerian businessmen. These properties had been bought at low prices, and the Algerians had then proceeded to cash in on them with a greed which fairly equalled that of their predecessors. During the months which followed the decrees of March, my government was called on to nationalize not only farms, but hotels, restaurants, cafés and business concerns, which had belonged to Algerians for a short time only.

We had never at any moment envisaged turning these nationalized properties into state-controlled concerns. It was up to the workers to elect their own managerial staff and direct their own undertakings. In the forum, democracy was no longer a formal political game, dominated by the money power, but had taken its place where it ought to be: at the foundations, on the actual working-sites, in the solid relationship between workman and production, and in the equitable distribution of profits. From now on, the state could only intervene in the process in the capacity of counsellor, regulator, or sleeping partner.

Autogestion would have produced problems even in France, which is a highly-developed country, as experience has proved that it is not easy to change over from a capitalist to a socialist economy. In an underdeveloped country like Algeria, it brought with it even more serious difficulties, because the inadequacy, both in quantity and in quality, of our trained personnel is striking. The spirit of individualism, of anarchy even, is very developed and our heads of undertakings are far too keen to adopt a feudal outlook, even when they have been elected to these posts. There were mistakes and abuses, gropings, and in some cases serious failures; we ourselves, in the light of experience, have had to modify our way of thinking and reshape some of our beliefs.

However, at the end of a year of *autogestion*, the balance was already on the credit side, in spite of the peevish diatribes of the western press, which had followed the progress of our experiment with the decided intention of crying failure at the first signs of difficulty. The question now arose of what to do with the profits from our nationalized enterprises. Our friends in the U.G.T.A.[1] considered that these profits should be paid into a fund for solving the unemployment problem. But I could not see that this was a very happy solution, either equitably or from the human point of view, and in the end I persuaded our friends to agree. The *fellah* earns 750 francs[2] a day on a farm, and already contributes a considerable part of it (23 per cent) to the *Caisse de Solidarité*.[3] How then could we expect him to pay a supplementary annual subsidy which did not apply to other people, such as government officials? On the other hand, it seemed absolutely essential to me that the *fellah* should feel that he is a producer, and no longer a mere wage-earner. By awarding him a yearly bonus, representing his share of the profits raised by his own enterprise, he would acquire tangible proof of his social progress.

I cannot pretend, of course, that *autogestion* as now practised in Algeria could not be improved upon. But it is important to distinguish between the two kinds of criticism of *autogestion*. One kind is made in all good

[1] *Union Générale des Travailleurs Algériens.*
[2] Tr. note: about eleven shillings and sixpence.
[3] Tr. note: the *Caisse de Solidarité* corresponds roughly to our National Insurance.

faith, with the intention of improving it. The other is peevish, spiteful, and entirely pessimistic; it comes from certain groups of Algerians and, through shortcomings and abuses, it is directed against the actual principle of control of the nation's assets by the people.

In fact, it is clear that the Algerian bourgeoisie obviously sees in *autogestion* a lost opportunity of doing business, and the end of those delectable prospects which it nurtured so shamelessly after the departure of the French. After the War of Independence had been won by the people, and by the people alone, the bourgeoisie of this country hoped to step into the shoes of the Europeans and to be the sole inheritors of their riches, leaving the people to their poverty.

I was able to forestall this plan, and in future I shall be on my guard. It has not escaped my notice that by their denigration of *autogestion*, the rich Algerians have betrayed their secret ambition to return to private enterprise and its unfair profits system. If their ambition were realized, it would be the end of socialism in Algeria, and consequently the end of the nation's independence. It would also be the end of hope for a better life which the Revolution has brought to a suffering people. He who attacks *autogestion*, either directly or indirectly, openly or covertly, violates the elementary rights of the masses, hoodwinks and betrays them, and stabs them in the back. As long as I live, and as long as I have any strength, I shall not allow anyone in Algeria to touch this most precious achievement of the Revolution.